OTHER BOOKS BY THE AUTHOR

The following titles are books by the author
*Fresh Anointing
*From Tears to Cheers
* Don't Give Up!
*Being an Uncommon Achiever
*Destined for Victory
*Fishing for Fruitfulness
*Candidate for the Throne
*Divine Enthronement
*Movement to the Next Level
*Sexual Crimes
*The Key to a Happy Home
*Changing You Story with You Act
*Conquest over Frustration
*7 Habits of Highly Ineffectual People
*Changing Your Darkness to Daystars*Understanding
the Four Phases of Life
*The Potency of Your Word
*The Race, the Rehearsals, the Ring

Social Issues
In Our
Generation

JOHNSON F. ODESOLA

authorHOUSE

AuthorHouse™
1663 Liberty Drive
Bloomington, IN 47403
www.authorhouse.com
Phone: 1 (800) 839-8640

Published by AuthorHouse 12/18/2019

ISBN: 978-1-7283-4003-6 (sc)
ISBN: 978-1-7283-4029-6 (e)

CONTENTS

ACKNOWLEDGEMENTS

In the compilation of this book, tailored for the exclusive use of those who desire to execute what the Scripture says, the Author referred to various renowned authorities, quotations of which has been minimized as much as is practicable.

The good authors of the renowned works mentioned are fully acknowledged for the relevance of their various pieces of work in their various fields.

My acknowledgement to Frank Colquhoun the man I have never met but his works and thoughts has greatly influenced my writing and view on contemporary issues of this time

PREFACE

As I was writing my lectures Manual for one of the Christian Colleges UK, a while ago in one of the night random thoughts was just running through my mind on crucial social concern or moral issue currently being experience in Africa as the case in developing countries: includes gender inequality, HIV/AIDS, Abortion, Homosexual, Divorce, drug abuse, oppression, poverty, limited access to health, sanitation, education facilities, food security etc. It is evident that the developing countries have serious social concerns in comparison to the developed world and the question in the developing countries is how to include these concerns within every sector of our life including religion and worship centers. However, regrettably, churches and leading Christian statesmen are avoiding facing the issue but reduce their activities and operation to worship centers and their personal empire. Then it occurs to me that you and I can think through them and stirred others to start thinking about those issues possibly we can together create something like a thesis for resolution.

My sincere concern in this writing is the main ethical issue, particularly with those of us who profess to be Christian and that we are obliged to face and resolve in the light of one faith. Many Christian have assimilated the anti-intellectual moods of today's world. They do not want to be told to use their minds, and they say. Some even declare it is 'unscriptural' to do so. In response I draw your attention to Paul injunction not to be conformed to the world but instead to "be transformed" by the renewing of our mind with a view to discerning God's pleasing and perfect will.

For instance it bordered me about when the church the salt of the earth in our continent will wake up to be what the Lord commissioned them to be. When you find out that in our continent where it is noised to be the present centre of revival is a place that is deficient in many basic things, just imagine the lack of infrastructures that has affected the manufacturing and production of goods and services especially in the third world. The export sector is dominated by the export of crude oil, Cocoa, coffee, tobacco, tea which have the disadvantage of not bringing in enough revenue. The same is true for gold, diamond, which is exported to Switzerland, Belgium, Britain and Dubai before Africans go there to buy the wedding rings and bracelets to sell. The necessary infrastructures and technologies needed are often completely absent. There are no gold and diamond cutting firms in Africa because the infrastructures do not exist. As a result the millions of jobs that gold and diamond cutting create are found in Israel, Belgium, Britain, US even though they do not mine these minerals. In Nigeria, Gabon, Equatorial Guinea, Angola, Chad all major oil producing countries, it is sad to note that lack of infrastructure has hampered expansion in the oil sector, leading to shortages of petroleum products, higher prices and queue forming seen in Nigeria, Ghana, Togo, Liberia, Tanzania, Zimbabwe, Somalia, Malawi, Zambia. There are few petrochemical industries in the continent due to lack of infrastructures. As a result most oil exports are in the crude form which brings in limited revenues.

The telecommunication including ICT sector is still struggling to catch up with the rest of the world. Internet connection is absent in the rural parts of the continent and connection is very slow in cities where internet is available. In many areas there are no fixed telephone lines and mobile telephone infrastructure is still at the infancy stage. Absence of telecommunication infrastructure is part of the reason why cost of running business is expensive in the continent compared to other regions. Schools, hospitals, banking and security operations are hampered by the absence of these vital infrastructures.

The agricultural sector is no exception. Farmers have no access to credits, improved seeds, tractors, irrigation facilities, fertilizers and silos and other storage facilities, and receive no support from government. Farming in Africa is dominated by the use of cutlasses/machetes, hoes and other rudimentary equipment. Despite the presence of major rivers and lakes lack of irrigation infrastructure has deadly hampered the agriculture sector. Farmers still rely on nature for rain in order to plant and farming is still at the subsistence level. As a result the average farmer can only produce to feed himself with little or nothing to sell. The result is the food shortage, high cost of food, hunger and the extreme poverty seen in Zimbabwe, Ethiopia, Niger and Mali, Burkina Faso, Sierra Leone and Somalia.

In most countries there are no proper housing infrastructures such as water, electricity and waste management not even in the capital cities. A visit to any village or town gives the same picture of poor and substandard housing and poor quality of public services and mortgage is a dream. They face constant barrage of water and energy disruptions with high utility bills as these sectors struggle to cope due to lack of infrastructure. The dwindling housing stock has forced people to live in slumps and engage in occupy-build-service instead of build-service-occupy. This explains why most residential areas lack running water, schools, electricity, clinics, toilets, playgrounds, car parks and access roads as there are no central planning authority to enforce building and zoning rules.

The education sector, the foundation of the continents development effort has its share of the infrastructure problems. The institutions lack modern facilities such as state of the art libraries, laboratory simulation facilities, studios, computers, books, staff bungalows, classrooms, students' accommodation and electricity. In most institutions it is still chalk, paper, and blackboard and there are no internet connections. The infrastructure problem has affected the quality and delivery of education in the continent. Of about 9,760 Accredited Universities in the World that were ranked, only University of Cape Town and University of Witwatersrand managed to place 179 and 319 positions respectively in the top 500. (Source: topuniversities.com/2008). Without the infrastructures the institutions are unable to produce the high quality of architects, engineers, planners, bankers, lawyers, doctors, teachers, nurses, technicians that the third world desperately need in this increasingly scientific and technological age. This explains why in most countries, major architectural and engineering works are undertaken by foreigners and foreign companies from USA, Japan, China and Europe. The Universities lack well trained lecturers and some of them are amateur in the use of computers, internet and podcasting all powerful tools essential to delivering quality education. In most universities students and lecturers have very limited access to electricity which limits their ability to conduct any meaningful academic work.

Whereas students in advanced countries get their hands on books immediately they are released those in third world have to wait several years to get the same books due to poor funding. Very few of our universities can boast of a million volumes of books in their libraries. Even the few books that exist are so old that information contained in them are valueless. This explains why there are no breakthroughs in our universities. Our research institutions have achieved very little because they are underfunded and lack the supporting accoutrements to carry out any meaningful research.

Increasing access to water, sanitation, roads, electricity, railways, trams, inland water transport system, airports, harbours, telecommunicate ion, canals, and providing improved seeds, credits, subsidies and irrigation infrastructures are essential to Africa's economic and social development, for without them it will be impossible to reduce poverty and improve both urban and rural lives. It is costly but the price is worth paying.

I cannot imagine a right minded Christian to fold arm and feel unconcerned as salt and light of the World. Most of the questions raised here are large ones and of a complex character. Certainly many of them do not permit of a simple, cut- and -dried answer from the Christian point of view, as we have done here, nor is it possible to deal with them adequately or satisfactorily within a short compass. The subject has been tackled the way we deemed best. It may not be a perfect work. The views expressed are results of pastoral experience and counseling in different continents, reading, researching, interview and interaction with people in different countries, culture and setting especially across sex, the older and the younger generation of our time. It is an attempt to answer the questions of moral issues, which is a reality of our time in a fair and honest manner with deep understanding of the various dynamic involved and to show that Christians especially those in leadership, Priest, Clergy, Pastors, Government officials, Editors, Farmers, Educates, Specialists, Expertrates, Senators and other progressively minded people should be prepare to come to grips with these difficult issues of our time. Every group and strata of people have something worthwhile to articulate about the issues at hand. Feel free to disagree with some of the issues raised so that we can both think through them for a better community and good life. Most of the issues goes beyond, one particular race or one particular denomination or organization. Many of the concern are not about personal ministry or personal kingdom or empire as we repeatedly have in these days, not about your personal revelations, sentiments or prejudices but about larger God's Kingdom.

Let us together think through the moral questions of our generation.

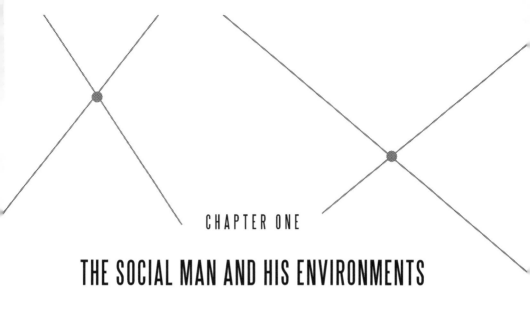

CHAPTER ONE

THE SOCIAL MAN AND HIS ENVIRONMENTS

In this chapter, we shall be considering a number of vital socio-cultural, political, moral and religion issues currently being experience in African countries, as a case in developing countries. These include the social man, his environment, gender inequality, HIV/AIDS, sex, marriage, divorce, abortion, homosexual, drug abuse, health, oppression, and poverty.

Does God Support Genetics Experiment?

The notion that the genetically composition of any organism - plant, animal or man - is somehow sacrosanct is based on both a theological and a scientific fallacy.

Biblical Reflections

In Genesis 1 and 2 we read that God made all living creatures 'according to their kind,' that they were good, and that Adam gave names to every 'kind' of animal. We are nowhere told in the Bible that the biological state of affairs existing at the time Adam was in Eden was to be unchanged for the rest of the world's history. There are many recorded examples of both extinction and intra-specific genetically charge which have nothing to do with human avarice and sin (ie the effects of the fall), but which have substantially changed the fauna and flora of many land in the past few centuries.

More important, it is naïve and incorrect to regard the 'image of God which distinguishes man from the animals (Genesis 1:27, 2:7) as related in any way to his biological characteristics. Only if God is literally a paternal monarch do we have to regard our head, hand, digestive system, and so on as made on the same pattern as his. In fact the Bible is at pains to emphasize God's transcendental divinity (ie Psalms 121:-4, John 4:24), and to distinguish this from the times he look human form (in various Old Testament Theophanies, and particularly as Jesus son of Nary). The New Testament writers repeatedly point out of the need of individual's repentance and faith, and the comparative irrelevance for salvation of heredity (e.g John 1:13; 1 Peter 1:22-23). Even the comparison by Paul of the effects of Adam's and Christ's death (Romans 5:12-17) does not necessary involve the genetically ancestry of Adam to the whole of the human race, since it is spiritual and not physical consequences that are the concern of Paul. In fact, Adam lived many years after his spiritual death in Eden (Romans 9:8). Our genes and chromosomes are a necessary part of our nature as body-souls, but our spiritually no more (or less) significant than our feet, eyes, ear or unpreventable parts' (1 Corinthians 12:14-26).

Science Worldview

Early work in radiation genetic apparently showed that the genetically materials was mystically stable, able to be charged (or mutated) only by high energy radiation. The discovery of chemicals which produce mutations and the realization that many cells are capable of repairing a considerable amount of genetically damage (the early mutation experiment were largely carried out on mature sperm which are metabolically almost inert) has led to a fuller interpretation: that the DNA and protein which make up the genes and chromosomes are just as reactive as similar molecules with deferent factions. The present understanding of the genetic content of an individual or group is that it undergoes continual change, but the most of the altered forms are eliminated by repair, cell death or reduces fertility. Ageing and many cancers are the results of the accumulation of genetically charges during life.

There are some people who regard all experiment or 'interference' with 'natural' processes as wrong. Such people regard any scientific research (or logically, medical treatment) as unwarranted trespassing on God's prerogative. They are of the same way of thinking as those who condemned Simpson for using chloroform during childbirth, since 'in pain (women) shall bring forth children' (Genesis 3:16) Simpson's rejoinder was to refer his critics to God's earlier use of a general anaesthetic in Genesis 2:21. However, Christian- particularly Protestant- tradition has always been on the side of enquiry as a means of understanding God's purposes better: thinking God's thoughts after him, in Kepler's phrase. Most of the founders of the Royal Society were Christian. Isaac Newton was more interested in eschatology than physics; As it was said, Rutherford caused the words 'Great are the works of the Lord, studied by all who have pleasure in them' (Psalms 111:2) to be carved over the entrance of the Cavendish Laboratory Cambridge; the discovery of the basic laws of genetics, Gregor Mendel, was an Augustinian abbot; and the tradition of scientific enterprise by Christians continues unabated.

Is there any particular danger in general experiment which may bring it under God's condemnation? Individual conscience must be the arbiter here: there are ethically sensitive areas in parts of genetic research where Christian involvement may do better by regulating than boycotting and condemnation.

On Reproduction

The techniques of artificial insemination, egg or zygote transfer, selective abortion of deformed foetus, etc., raise several issues: a woman may bear a child carrying neither her husband's genes nor her own. This may be construed as adultery, but since her marriage was primarily designed for social and not sexual purposes (Genesis 2:18), decisions about the morality of these techniques are better based on whether or not the participants are dehumanized, ie reduced to the to the status of mere machines rather than the integrated body-mind-spirit that we are designed to be by God. A similar criterion can be applied to experiment on foetal tissue; an embryo which has no chance of developing to be a 'person' may conscientiously be used for research which may lead to the prevention of future deformity or alleviation of suffering. Notwithstanding, babies born to a couple who are not its genetic parents are technically illegitimate.

Arguments are increasingly being advanced that particular couples with a high risk of producing abnormal children should not reproduce because of the burden that their offspring will place upon society. Although this is a valid factor in any decisions that are made (Amos 5:11), it is more important to consider the personal suffering of any child that might be born, and its effects of the family, including other children.

Differences in Race

Different populations differ genetically. It has been claimed that it is degrading to study the differences because some people (or groups or races) might be humiliated in comparison with others. This is nonsense; God has a role for each one of us, and it is better to know each other innate capabilities of different people than falsely (and theologically) assume all men are identical (Matthew 25:14-30, Mark 4:8, 1 Corinthians 12:27 ff, etc.).

Microbial Drug Resistance

Disease-causing organisms fairly rapidly evolve resistance to drugs. Unfortunately the genes conferring resistance can sometimes be transferred to other micro-organisms, including some which are normal and usually harmless inhabitants of the gut. The mechanisms of transfer between forms, and the possibility of incorporation useful properties in strains lacking them (such as the ability to make missing enzymes in the cells of people who are inherently incapable of synthesizing them) has led to much profitable research and hope for diseased people. It is possible that virulent disease organism might be produce and propagated as a result. The chance of this happening is a subject for expert argument; many scientists think the risk is negligible if appropriate safeguards are taken and the whole subject is now a matter for governmental control.

Ethical unease about genetic experiment probably stems from a belief that genes are sacred objects, fundamental to creation. They are not. There are a variety of problems which may arise from research in genetics, but their solution will come from the application of general principles or responsibility towards nature rather than from any special pleading or anathematic.

Are We Really Responsible For the Environment?

The enormous increase of scientific knowledge in the past two to three hundred years has led to a general understanding of how the world works. And a corresponding decrease in the mysterious areas which our ancestors too often envisaged was the place for God. Plough Sunday, Harvest Festival and the like were occasions for homage to a Supper-Farmer capable of withholding blessing from the unwary. As God became confined more and more to the gap in our knowledge, theologians (both evangelical priests and catholic mystics) were forced to explain his activities as almost wholly spiritual. A rediscovery of the biblical doctrine of creation and its implications for the relationship of God to the world has long been necessary. It became critical with the growing awareness in recent years of pollution, over-population, and resource depletion.

Man's Authority Over Nation

According to Genesis 1:28 God gave to man he had created in his image dominion over all over the living creatures. This authority has been taken by many Christians down the ages as the mandate to use both the living and inorganic worlds as God's gift for exploitation. This in turn has attracted the accusation that our environmental problems are the direct consequence of Christian teaching. This is often a fair comment.

For example, the seventeenth-century Puritans regarded New England as their promised land – a sanctuary from their Egypt, a testing ground, and a meeting place with God. Since Eden was a garden, they assumed that the reduction of wildness to garden (and, incident, through the gospel) was a proper Christian task. To them, wild country was basically immoral: the hostility of nature to man was obvious - in flood and drought, forest and desert. Any action taken to bring wilderness into cultivation or, by labour, to exploit natural resources, partook of quality of virtue. It was in terms of this Puritan wilderness-to-garden ethic that the advance of the frontier westward across America took place.

A comparable colonial master, example was the so call improvement of some specific land in their colonies in the first half of the nineteenth century, involving the clearance of the certain inhabitants to the coast or part of the colonies. In almost all the cases this was supported by the local ministers. To conquer and control nature in such circumstances was no more than obedience to God's original command.

The Caretaker

This interpretation of the creation ordinance is a classic example of taking scripture out of its context. Since man is made in God's image, this means that he (we) must exercise reliability and responsibility. (The facile understanding that man has God's image through the possession of head, hands, legs etc. is ridiculous, John 4:24). Consequently the dominion exercised by man is not to be an anthropocentric plunder of God's gifts to him, but rather a responsible stewardship of God's own world.

Most of the Bible teaching about the environment is in the Old Testament, but on several occasions Christ confirmed our mandate to work with the natural world in the role of a manager or steward, responsible as it were to a non-executive director. For example Jesus uses the analogy of absentee landlord for God (Luke 12:42-48, 19:12-27, 20:9-18, etc.) In other places the New Testament pictures man in his relation to nature as a shepherd, a farm manager or a household stewards.

We have a God given role to care for natural recourses on behalf of our Lord – a role which allows us to make use of the resources for our own needs, but does not permit us to destroy them since they are entrusted to us only for a limited period. Man with nature is like a library-user: entitled and expected to make the best use of the contents, but trusted to handle the books property so that they are available to others.

Divine Duty

When we recognize that our treatment of our physical surrounding is linked to our spiritual obedience in God the creator, the Old Testament pledges the Promised Land yielding bountiful if the Israelites behaved themselves make sense (Leviticus 26:3-5, Isaiah 24:5) to modern ears by linking of agricultural yield to moral behaviour sounds odd, its only when we appreciate that both biological and purposive causes make sense in God who holds them together (Colossians 1:17) that we appreciate this paradox. It was the Israelites disobedience in failing to take possession of the whole of the Promised Land (Judges 1:27-33) that produce over-crowding and fighting, and led to havoc in the fragile ecosystem (growing conditions) of the eastern Mediterranean lands.

Our response to environment must not be to neglect it as neutral, nor to hallow it as divine, but to use it as part of our spiritual duty. Indeed only if we see the world about us as God's good world, will we be able to involve ourselves with environment problems with the responsibility as urgent as, say, teaching or evangelism (Romans 9:20-22). We are agents for

God's purpose on earth. We fail if we attempt to discharge ourselves through church activities or Christian involvement in the usual sense of that phrase; and we fail equally if we sentimentalize pigs and primroses. There Israelites were placed by God in the easily upset ecology of Palestine. Now that the world has filled with people, it has become almost as vulnerable ('a fragile space - ship). No longer can we run away from environmental problems like our forebears, because there is nowhere to escape to. Our only hope is to accept the charge lay upon us in the in the first chapter of the Bible.

Man's Conscience and His Social Behaviour

'So always let your conscience be your guide.' That is how the old song put it and it is fine up to a point. But it is not the whole story. We must be clear what we mean when we speak of 'conscience'; because a Christian understanding of it differs from that suggested by the way people often speak. My conscience is clear 'implies a final verdict of innocence; but is that necessarily true? Is it invariably infallible? Do we all possess this kind of inbuilt moral compass? People sometimes say of someone, 'He has got no conscience at all,'

Although the actual word only occurs a few times in the Bible, mainly in Paul's letter, the idea is present throughout. 'A pure heart' implies much the same thing (Psalms 24:4). This purity of heart depends upon awareness of good and evil. Consequently for the Israelite the observance of the law was the guarantee of a clear conscience, because here God had shown what was required of man. But even this was not enough. Job was convinced of his righteousness (Job 27:6) until he came face to face with God (Job 42:5-6). Here is something much more profound. The ultimate secret of a clear conscience is closeness to God. Outwards observance of the law is not enough - the Lord looks upon the heart. Thought and motive count with God as well as outwards behaviour. This was what the Pharisees had failed to understand (Matthews 15:2) and it was the turning- point for Saul of Tarsus when he reflected on the command, 'You shall not covet' (Romans 7:7).

Restriction of Conscience

This is not to say that only those who belong to God's people and possess his written law have an operative conscience. Paul explains that Gentiles too show same awareness of God's law and their conscience bears witness to the fact (Romans 2:14 – 16). All men, made in God's image, have a moral sense given by God, however much they may abuse it. By itself it is inadequate. It needs the further enlighten on what God has revealed in the law. Still more, under the new covenant, this law of God is to be re-writing on men's hearts by the spirit (Hebrews 8:10). By this means the conscience is enlivened and man is empowered by the Holy Spirit to observe the spirit of God's law as well as the letter. So Paul can say confidently, 'God is my witness', in order to support what he is claiming: his conscience is clear. Uniquely in Jesus we find that absolute purity of conscience that that only sinlessness and total obedience can provide (John 8:29).

From what has been said we can see that conscience is not by itself an autonomous and infallible guide for our social behaviour. My conscience may not be accusing me when I deserve it, because I am not fully aware with God's law or am out of touch with the living God. But every man has a conscience and a duty not to act against it.

'Pangs' of conscience accurately express the biblical teaching about it, for this pain is an internal effect of God's wrath against sin (Romans 1:18). This is the pain felt after the commission of sin; but, as in a game when the light flashes on after you have missed the target, so the conscience only registers after failure. Its role is negative; indicating that some transgression has occurred. Of course it may register also in anticipation as the 'mind' toys with the possibility of the certain course of action, but the New Testament distinguishes these two things (Romans 2:14-15). While the 'conscience' is basically negative and retrospective, the 'mind' is able also to deliberate on choices beforehand.

A Branded Conscience

On many matters of social behaviour there is clear and explicit direction on the Bible; for the Christian the right course is obvious. But what about those innumerable areas where there is no precise instruction in the Bible? As we progress in the Christian life our conscience should became more sensitive to what is right because it is better informed. We are not to be 'squeezed' into the world's mould' (Romans 12:2) the principles of conduct laid down in the Bible change our attitude as we begin more to see things through Christ's eyes. One might imagines that this means that we will tend always to become increasingly rigid and inflexible, but that is not the case. Whilst our moral standards ought to be continually rising, we should also discovering a new liberty -a freedom from man-made rules and superstition by which we were once enslaved.

Now this kind of slavery is much common amongst Christians than we usually care to admit. The man who has been delivered from this Paul calls 'strong' but the man with a 'weak' conscience has not yet achieved this understanding and freedom (Romans 15:1, 1 Corinthians 8:7). Therefore as a person matures spiritually, so his conscience may disallow some things that once were unquestioned and permit other things that previously were disapproved. So if conscience develops in this way, it will never provide itself a consisted pattern of guidance for my social behaviour. My own attitude will change over the years concerning some of these greyer areas of conduct.

Regards For Others

There is another factor here also. I have no right to lay down the law for anyone else beyond the clear teaching of scripture, any more than I should allow someone to do the same for me. To our own master we stand or fall. Paul is insistent that our own liberty and enlighten should never be allowed to damage someone else's conscience. To ride rough-shod over their moral sensitivity, even if it be ill-informed and the work of a 'weak' conscience, is to flout the higher law of love for any Christian brother. Love is superior to liberty. My new- found freedom must never be allowed to harm the conscience of another for whom Christ died. Consequently I may find it necessary at times to deny myself certain liberties that I firmly believe that are fully permissible for myself for the sake of my 'weaker brother,' lest I encourage him to act against his conscience to his own detriment (1 Corinthians 8:13).

Take, for example, the question of smoking. Is it right for me? Obviously the Bible has nothing direct to say. It is expensive – but so are many other little indulgences. It is bad for the health -but so, we are told, are all animal fats. It is habit-forming -but so is tea drinking. It is anti-social -but it supporters would claim the opposite. You can argue the toss endlessly. In the end each one must decide honestly for himself without writing off those who may disagree. It's the same with drinking. Drunkenness is a terrible scourge, but wine is said to 'make glad the heart of man.' Can I control my own appetites? Could my example lead others astray? Or would a very negative attitude on my part unnecessarily confirm people's identification of Christianity with moral taboos? Let each one of us be fully persuaded in his own mind. And my loving concern for other people should keep me open to a change in my own behaviour in a different social situation.

A final word of warning

If we repeatedly act against our conscience, it will cease to function as it ought. It may become defiled (Titus 1:15) and even cauterized to the extent to the extent of complete insensitivity (1Timothy 4:2). That is to travel in the reverse direction of God's purpose, for he wishes us to lives so close to him that our conscience is clear and un-condemning. But even then, when no pangs are felt, The Christian knows that the final judge of his conduct is not his conscience but God (1 Corinthians 4:4).

On Racial Prejudice And Security Revenge

'Race is explosive subject'! Almost any group of people can get involves in an animated debate on race - principles, prejudice, denunciation and passionate concern flying in all directions. When it was suggested in the newspaper that we must accept that ours is now a society permanently characterized by a multiplicity of creeds, racial origins and ethnic identities, there were some bitter reactions in reply. One correspondent asked if the writer had any ideal of the hate and tension building up among many white people in the West. On the other side, a publication such as Race Today gives expression to the anger and bitterness of many in the so call Black community. I am yet to meet a black and white person except the fact that those who invented this idea are colour blind.

Race and colour are not just problem for one country but all nations. They are issues of world-wide significance. Through our newspapers and on our television screens we see evidence of racial conflict, we know of the evils that result from apartheid in South Africa. Take for instance the scene in America: When John Fitzgerald Kennedy was elected the president in 1960 many conservative white folk of Anglo-Saxon background refused to accept him as their president. To them Kennedy was Irish and, as such, a subhuman being and that were all there was to it. They did not accept his presidency until he died. The same phenomenon is going on with Obama. To certain white folk he is not human enough and they would never accept him as their president. Even if he stands on his head and does the right thing they would not accept him as a human being. In Russia persons of dark complexion, even those from the Caucasus, such as Turks, are routinely killed by Russian youths. African students in Russia dare not show their faces in the public at night, certainly not in certain parts of Russia or they are beaten up or even killed.

Somehow it bothers me that many Africans only talk about their internal politics and refuse to concern themselves with larger issues that could affect them. These days Africans goes to the Europe or USA and pretend that everything is okay. In the early 1900s when the French man Simon Binnet invented his IQ testing it was found that Slavic Europeans (Poles, Czechs, Ukrainians, Russians, Serbs, Croats etc) scored lower than Western Europeans by exactly fifteen points (Western Europeans, that is, Frenchmen, Germans, Spanish, Italians, Scandinavians etc share similar Western culture with Americans). The US Congress passed legislation banning Slavs from coming to America for they were deemed an inferior race! (At present Africans tend to score by exactly fifteen points below white folk in IQ tests, but their children born the US who are acculturated to white America tend to do as well as white children. That is to say that the so-called IQ difference is cultural rather than genetic. People, black and white, are ninety nine point nine the same.)

Asians were banned from obtaining American citizenship in 1898. It was later when it was discovered that when Slavs stayed in the USA long enough to be acculturated that their children tend to do as well as Anglo Saxons that Congress reversed the banning.

Most Africans actually do not know that it was only in the 1960s that Congress finally allowed non-Western Europeans to become US citizens! It was only in 1969 that the Supreme Court ruled against so-called miscegenation laws (laws banning interracial marriages ...thus, the brothers claim that the marriage between an African man, Obama sr, and a white woman was illegal hence his son, Barack, is not really a legal American) There are whites who are so convinced that black folk are unintelligent that they are in shock that Americans voted for a black man as their president. They cannot accept that an inferior African and his slave wife are in their white house, sleeping on the bed that their leaders slept on! To them this is desecration. It gives them the apoplexy.

A whole lot of crazy things have happened in this globe and could happen again; that we do not as yet, live in a colour-blind society! Or live in the nonsense which some call a post- racial society. Racists are alive and well, and sadly, in huge numbers! Here is a great world question about which Christian need to do some pretty fast and through thinking. What is required of us by the Gospel?

Bible Teachings

First, we need to understand correctly the teaching scriptures and not be misled by those who wrest its teachings to justify attitudes of racial superiority or policies of separate development. For instance, the curse of Noah Genesis 9:29 has been used by certain theologian to justify the perpetual subjection of black to white, where as its application is clearly to the Canaanites who were of the same Semitic stock as the Hebrews. And some white people (who would be the first to pride in the expansion of our stock and culture across the world) use St Paul's words at Athens (Acts 17:26) to justify keeping coloured people in their own countries and out of ours, whereas the whole drift of St Paul's sermon is 'the complete antithesis of an exclusive, nationalistic, racist spirit'.

When we look at the Bible, teaching us a whole, we see that it is set in a universal context. All men, it proclaims, are made in the image of God. All are sinners. Christ died for all men. Christians of all races are one in Christ. It is a known fact, that many Old Testament passages do suggest a narrow Jewish particularize vis-à-vis neighboring peoples, but the story does not end there. As we follow its sweep we see that the prophets repeatedly condemned a nationalism that forget justice and mercy to the poor and the stranger within the gates and called God's people to be a light to the nations, that his salvation may reach to the end of the earth (Isaiah 49:6). The New Testament rejoices in the breaking down by Christ of the middle wall of partition between Jew and Gentile and it closes with St John the seer's splendid vision of the City of God, by whose light the nations shall walk and into which their glory and splendor shall be brought (Revelation 21:24-26)

This question is also asked about Africa because it is the poorest continent on earth. It is a continent where for 30 years there has not been any concrete economic development compared to the rest of the world. It lags behind all the other continents in terms of economic and social development. Most if not all the countries African continent have similar economic problems namely high unemployment, high inflation, higher deficits, poor state of economic and social infrastructures including roads, harbours, education, airports, telecommunication, health and sanitation and rail system. Africa is a continent where people die for lack of food, water, and against common preventable diseases. It is a continent full of misery, desperation and hopelessness. It is a continent where very few children under the age of five survive the menace of the six killer diseases. It is a continent where people have no access to basic necessities of life. It is a continent where people walk several miles for water and children have no access to education and medical services. It is a continent where rural life is nothing but a condemnation to abject poverty. It is a place where people live in mud/thatched houses with bamboo/raffia leaves as roofing sheets. It is a continent full of wars and armed conflicts. It is a continent of dictators and kleptocrats, a continent where corruption is rewarded and achievement is shunned, a continent where entry into public life/service is seen as a means to acquiring wealth and a means of getting top positions. It is a continent where life expectancy is low and corruption very high.

So is it a colour or race thing? I must say that I do not agree or subscribe to the notion that poverty has any colour inferring in it and that the underdevelopment and impoverishment which is prevalent on the African continent is deeply rooted in centuries of slavery and colonialism, coups, armed conflicts, brain drain, endemic corruption and mismanagement, dictatorial rule, Kleptocracy, foreign interventions and the fight for control of the natural resources.

Historical Perspective

As John Stott (2006:270) rightly says it is not possible to jump straight to contemporary examples of racism in Europe and America, and ignore the evils of slavery and the slave trade out of which it has largely sprung. It has been said that no sensitive American can confront issues arising from ethnicity in the US today without looking back beyond the civil war to the cruelty and degradation of life on the plantations.

It is generally accepted that "the slave has three defining characteristics: his person is the property of another man, his will is subject to the owner's authority and his labour or services are obtained through coercion (David Brion 1966:31) Being regarded as nothing but property, slaves were normally deprived of elementary human rights: e.g., the right to marry or to own or bequeath possessions or to witness in a court of law. Although

14

slavery of different kinds and degrees was universal in the ancient world, it is inexcusable that the professedly

Christian nations of Europe (Spain and Portugal, Holland. France and Britain) should have used this inhuman practice to meet the labour needs of the New World colonies. Worse still, practicing Christians developed an elaborate but false defense of slavery on several grounds.

* Social and economic necessity, since there was no other source of labour in the colonies to provide raw material for the Industrial Revolution in Europe.
* Ethnicity superiority, since Negros deserved no better treatment.
* Biblical permission, since scripture regulates but not condemns slavery.
* Humanitarian benefits, since the trade transferred slaves from African savagery to American civilization.
* Missionary opportunity, since African "infidels" would be introduced to Christianity in the New World.
* The blatant rationalization of slave-owners makes one blush with embarrassment today. Now looking back at history over the last 200 years; colonial masters have emigrated in their thousands to new land (after fighting the original inhabitants). Before Wilberforce, westerner was deeply involved in the slave trade from Africa to North America, and the Caribbean.

Throughout the remainder of the 19th Century she painted large parts of the map of the world red. The Empire supplied colonial imperialist with cheap raw materials for manufacture and the finished product were then exported to the world at great profit. Colonial masters showed that wealth and power were to be found in Britain. For so many years even the church fostered the idea of making Britain the motherland of the people they colonized. This is almost a forgotten issue now in some parts of Africa because of advent of Africa Independent Churches (AIC).

Furthermore, in the period of shortage of labour after the war, Britain actively encourage people from those countries they colonized to come into their country to do the less desirable jobs (even going so far as to set up recruiting centers in some places). Britain actually invited people to come and many are doing jobs that other people will not do. For instance, transportation and health services in Britain would have collapse without the help of the Commonwealth immigrants.

What about the East African Asians? Well, when Kenya, Uganda and Tanzania became independent, Britain gave those people opportunity of retaining British nationality if they did not wish to apply for citizenship in the new nations. Britain is in honour bound to accept those expelled from East Africa who hold British passport and have nowhere to go.

On any realistic understanding of this situation then, we must accept that from now on, there will be a colour mixture population of some two million or so within the fifty million inhabitant of Great Britain and this should be same pattern in any of the viable develop or developing democratic Government in the world.

What should our attitude be to each other? In the light of the basic teaching in the Bible; we can have no doubt about the answer. We cannot treat as second-class citizens those who, whatever their colour, share the humanity which the Son of God took upon him in the Incarnation and which he has redeemed by dying for us.

The Christian Responsibility

In consequences, Christian citizens in this nation and in the other countries of the world have great responsibilities laid upon them. First, we must get to know the facts about legislation and other official action designed both to restrict immigration and to ensure justice to all. We should learn too about the various and conflicting pressures of public opinion which lie behind these action. We need to know also the truth in contrast to the parrots cries about immigrants coming to live off Britain social security system and the calls that they should be encouraged, if not pressurized, to return home. Also the issue of African for African the case for Zimbabwe with farmers and the dictatorship Government was a sure one. For example it is a fact that many have no homes outside Zimbabwe which many of the younger generation have been born and brought up here and know no other country. We must be ready to speak up and be counted when the so called enlightened communities which pride themselves on having no race problem, show themselves acutely racist. That may well require of us individually some self-examination first!

Then we have positive responsibilities towards new Africa, new Briton etc. We should behave towards them with the same courtesy and good neighborliness that we show people of our own race. We should take time and trouble to build bridges of understanding. We could visit a Roman Catholic, Baptist, Anglican, and Presbyterian churches or invite their priests to our homes. We should keep watch on policies in our area in regards to Job opportunities, housing, education etc and be ready to writer to local Government, supporting a local community project etc. In these days of pressure groups, Christians in city or town should stand together and when necessary challenge their senators, member of house of parliament or the local chancellors when injustice occur.

What part should the church at the national or local level for playing? It should be a shining example of a Christian fellowship which rises about the restricted outlook of a particular section of society (most often top class and middle-class). In Christ name, it should work for a nation in which all receive just and equal treatment and all can bring their particular contribution to the enrichment of the whole community. For instance, are we ready to make buildings available for Christians whose forms of worship may suggest 'Pentecostal pandemonium' rather than our own more sedate and traditional ways? Are we prepared to allow our premises to be used for the social gathering of people of other faiths - and in so far as conscience is allows, for religious purposes? Would we consider selling a redundant church building to such a group? Or are we just a replica of society an "in" group, protecting our special privileges, our property and position, against threats from those outside?

What about evangelism. Is that not our first and major responsibility? Perhaps we have something to learn here from General Booth. As he viewed the vast areas of poverty of Britain great cities with their disinherited and un-churched masses, he set out his order in the slogan - soup, soap and salvation. It is only as our congregations are seen to be servants of the community, ready to minister to the local situation in any way they can, that the message they proclaim has any possibility of being heard. Only if, like our Master, we are ready not to be ministered to but to minister and to identify at whatever cost with those who too often get a raw deal in our society, shall we commend the saving Gospel of Jesus Christ and open the way to response.

Is The Scripture Still Suitable For Making Moral Judgement Again In This Generation? Making moral judgments in today's world is far from being easy. The complexities of modern life can make moral decision-making about as intricate a work picking a route through the crowded streets of a large city. Add the fact that many of these decisions have to be taken on the spur of the moment and clear moral sign post become essential. So where are we to find them?

The answer that spring most easily the Christian's mind is in the Bible. The Bible is God's word. As Christians, we believe that God still speaks to through it its pages. It is to the Bible, there for that we turn first for guidance in the moral problems we meet.

Natural and right though this approach is, we soon find that the Bible does not provide us with clear answer to all the questions we want to ask about morality. The Christian who pins his faith in the scriptures as an 'enquire within on everything 'will certainly find some of his moral queries cleared up immodesty. But in other cases the solution may not be quite so obvious. In fact, there are three main grounds on which the Bible's usefulness as a moral guide-manual has been challenged by it critics.

Three Main Challenges

It Is Archaic

No one in his right mind would borrow a nineteenth-century road map to find his own way through a hyper- modern world network of trunk roads and motorways. How, then, can it be right to rely for moral guidance on a book that is not just one hundred but over two thousand years ago?

If we protest that the Bible is inspired by God- and he is every bit as alive today as he was in Old Testament time- we will have to reckon with the possibility that all the rules and guidelines he laid down for people in Bible times are meant to apply to us today. The Bible talks about seething kids in their mother's milk and woman keeping silence in church (Exodus 23:19, 1 Timothy 2: 11, 12) - the kind of issues which leave most of this generation readers puzzled, if not faintly amused.

It Is Not Applicable

When it comes identifying the Bible's teaching on a particular subject, a concordance is a very useful tool. But no concordance contains words like 'strike' 'euthanasia' 'pill' 'abortion' Nuclear weapon or H-bomb.' On this and many other moral issues which make the headline of today's papers, the Bible is apparently silent.

Even on these scriptures does highlights; its teaching is not always immediately relevant to the specific issue modern people face. The Old Testament, for example, encourages large families and demands capital punishment for rebellious teen-agers (Genesis1: 28; 24: 60; Psalms127: 4-5; Deuteronomy21: 18-21). Though such rules and such guidelines might have been considered right for an under populated world where there were a few means for dealing with violent social misfits, it is not nearly so obvious that they provide adequate guidance for Christians making their minds up on family planning and the death penalty today.

It Is Irrelevant

In his letter to the Romans, Paul write about people who do not read their Bibles but who still have moral standards and principles. Even those who live without the guidance of God's written law, he says, have that law; 'written on their hearts'.

Modern life provides ample evidence that Paul was right, 'there are plenty of people without a vestige of Christian faith who fight racial discrimination carry banner in antiabortion marches, deplore pornography, shun religion bigotry and are outraged by mugging. You do not have to be regular Bible reader to have standards, so why do need the Bible to give us guidance, when we all have this inbuilt (and Christian would say 'God given') sense of right and wrong anyway?

The criticism sounds plausible enough. But each has a compelling answer.

Importance of the Bible for Our Generation

It clears our moral vision

It is true that everyone has a sense of right and wrong. But, even in the best of us, that in build moral sense has been blurred and distorted by sin. If we want to something badly enough, our minds will convince us that black is white. If we do it after enough even our consciences will stop giving out there warning signals. Making moral judgment unaided is like insisting on driving up a busy motorway at high speed with a misted up windscreen.

The Bible is god's own demister. It answers the most basic questions anyone can ask about morality. 'What is good' and 'what is right'?

Good qualities, according to the Bible, 'are those we were reflected in God's character. For example if we are tempted to think that hoarding, or putting our own interest first, are not altogether bad traits, one grace at God's character as the Bible reveals it to us will be enough to set us back on course. And the right thing to do, according to the Bible, it is always the thing that is in line with God's will (Romans 12:2; Hebrews 13:21). As we read the scriptures; we are constantly pointedly to the line God's will takes in small things as well as big, and this pointers sign-post post us to right moral judgment in our own live.

We need the Bible as our ship's captain needs is radar in a sea fog. To pretend that it is unnecessary is as stupid is as dangerous as it would be for un airline pilot to switch off his automatic system and communicate with control tower as he comes in to land on poor visibility.

It points us to main-line principle

It is true that the Bible does not offer made-to measure solutions for every moral dilemma. But it does set out to achieve something for more important.

Every contemporary moral issue raises fundamental questions of right and wrong which sometimes lurk just below the surface. The abortion issue for example, is not just about back- street operators and clinic touts. It is about much more basic things – like the right of the foetus, the true nature of compassion, and the sanctity of human life. And on this bed-rock matter the Bible has plenty to say and many clear directives to give.

To criticize the scripture as inadequate then just because they do not include the vocabulary of the modern media, is far too shallow a reaction. The absence of the jargon forces us to look really big issue that lies below the surface of the contemporary debate. And to be made to dig down to that foundation level is a very healthy antidote to have decision making-making. The Bible stimulates us to work out moral judgments that are really sound- because they are based on main line principles.

In much the same way it is short-sighted to discard the Bible as a guidebook just because, on those occasions when it is specific, it sometimes deals with problems that are no longer of much concern. Underlying every one of the specific directive scripture offers is the main-line principles that are as relevant today as it was ever was. For instance, behind the law on building roof-parapets (Deuteronomy 22: 8) lies the principle of public safety. And the ban on seething the kid in its mother's milk illustrated the respective attitude men should have at all-time towards animal. Here we have main-line principles which have very clear application to life today.

To make these claims is not just to counter the charge that the Bible is teaching is inadequate and outdate. To find adequate solutions to modern moral issues it is essential to distinguish the main principle at stake. And the Bible serves as a unique contemporary guide book simply because it directs us to those principles and gives us God's mind on them.

It direct us to the source of moral power

In any moral dilemma, making the right decision is only stage one. Stage two-carrying the decision into practice - is much harder. For example, we do not really need any to tell us that generosity is right and bad-temperedness wrong; but in practice we know we are sometimes stingy and concessionary lose our temper. In other words, we lack the will- power to carry through the decision we make quite sensibly in our mind. At this level the Bible offers us a unique source of help. Some books on morality will convince us that we ought to live better lives. A few may even inspire us to make greater efforts. But in pointing us to the Almighty God the scripture do far more than that. They direct us to the source of moral power which can overcome our weakness and make us free to do the right thing as well as avoid the wrong. Some people caricature the Bible as Books which is full of 'Thou shall not's.' That is unfair, In fact, its central message is the triumphant 'You can- in God's power' (Philippians 4:13).

So the Bible is more than a guide book. It is God's power tool. Reading it regularly and obediently is like living with a piece of radio-active materials in your pocket -though rather more health! Through the Scripture God's can break habits, change attitudes and reinforce wills (Philippians 2:13).

Over and above information and discernment in making moral judgment, we badly lack this power to make our decision effective. The Bible directs us to the power source we need to convert our good intention to action. There is no more cogent argument to drive us back to the Bible as our uniquely relevant, adequate and necessary guide in living the moral life.

Can I Impact My Local Community

The Christian, because he worship the God of justice, does not shut his eyes to those things in the environment which are complained of; but at the same time sees that the immigrant in any country is a human being too. Nothing he says or does must deny the human dignity of the people around him, all of whom were made in the image of God.

The task of reconciliation and understanding is laid on the Christians shoulder by his faith. Of course he finds plenty of other people in the social field who are equally concerned, but there is no doubt that a Christian presence makes a different all its own. As one non- Christian social worker said to a pastor in Zimbabwe about a churchless area, 'There is no presence there.' He believes this made a difference to the very atmosphere. Of course it must since a group of people who pray affects the very place it is in.

Jesus saw this function of his people quite clearly. He said in the Sermon on the Mount that we are the salt of the world. He went on to spell this out. Salt, he said give savour. He was not speaking of preventing corruption but of giving things salty tang. That is the kind of impact he wanted his followers to have on society. The source of our saltines is God's law and the prophets.

Making an Impact

Of course there are problems when Christian exerts an influence on the local community. Christian compassion demanded the response the

Crypt founder the Reverend Dennis Downham made, but it was contrary to how ordinary people felt.

Perhaps one of the most direct ways of making an impact on the local community is by entering politics. One clergyman I know did this when ask to be a Senator for his senatorial division in his state. It meant his joining whatever party sponsoring him and accepting its discipline. There can be few politicians who have not at some time or another faced the clash between personal conviction and Party loyalty. The clergyman in question will find this to be true in full measures, I am sure, But meanwhile he can have I say in the central councils of the ruling party in his country, so the 'salt' should be able to operate there. Landlord associations flourish or stagger along in many areas today. A Christian friend of mine is one of the key officers in one of such group in his area. It is an opportunity to care for other people in the sort of practical ways that God expect us to do. Big organization make for increasing dehumanization and the local tenants' association is a way of off-setting this. Of course one is faced with the abrasive manner in which this world's children conduct their affairs so often. Some of the bitterness of public meetings can make one want to run away and keep out of it. But how will the 'salt' reach the food it is meant to savour if it stays in the cruet? A Christian in the right place at the right time can strengthen people of moderate persuasion and get things done peacefully.

Protesting

Here and there, as Christians are engaged with other citizens in the affairs of the locality, the chance to witness for Christ and his laws does come. It may be done very clearly when we meet outside a local cinema to witness to the goodness of human love and sexuality against pollution and exploitation going on inside. It may be when, as another Christian friend of mine has done, we get to work on the degrading material displayed in the newsagents. But in such cases we act first as citizens out of love for our neighbour. Gospel witness may or may not occur.

Michael Green, Choose Freedom (IVP)

CHAPTER TWO

SEX AND MARRIAGE

Sex and marriage are two vital issues that need critical postulations. In this chapter, I will address major sexual and marital questions that needs right answers. These critical questions are address below:

Sex Before Marriage

Falling in love is unforgettable experience. One day life seems to be going on in much the usual way and the next-well the poets and the songwriters have tried to capture the champagne feeling but, honestly, can you put it in words?

Our society, so it would seem, is obsessed with sex. Most popular magazines, modern films, numerous television programs, many commercial adverts and part of the music industry are bluntly designed to arouse and 'play on' our sexual urges and desire.

Put the two together - sex and falling in love - and you've got the most explosive potential known to man (feminists please add' and woman'). Think of the agony and the ecstasy of it, the pain and the pressure. 'Oh, have you been in love, me boy oh, have you felt the pain,' sang John McCormack years ago. And he went on,' I'd be sooner be in jail me-self than be in love again.'

Christian, being human, are no different from anybody else when it comes to the experience of sex and falling in love.' If you prick us, do we not bleed?' complained Shylock on behalf of his fellow Jews. So, too, we feel our sexuality and its potency just as much as anyone else and we'd be in a much worse states if we didn't. There is nothing wrong, about feeling the power of erotic love and its physical and emotional aspects.

The more I dig into the Bible the more I convinced I become that the God of all the earth is pro-sex. If you are looking for anti-sex information or ammunition, you will not find it in God's book. God created it, Paul reminds us in 1 Timothy 4:4 or as David also expresses it (Psalms 139:13-15 L.B). The Bible is never anti-sex. You will find nothing negative in it about the act of sexual intercourse itself. In fact, it language in describing the sex act is extravagant and views it as a celebration. However, pre-marital sex is immoral regardless of what the current thinking might be. Being in love constitutes no grounds and is certainly no condition for pre-marital sex. The only condition for a sexual relationship is marriage. A sexual relationship other than with your husband or wife is either perversion or adultery and fornication. If you refrain from sex at this time in your life when your physiological desires are at their height, you would have demonstrated discipline restraint, trust and respect, all of which crucial to a successful marriage. Here is why: In marriage you and your wife will normally see each other every day, but there are still those periods when you will be apart. You may be on business trip or one of you may be physically ill or your wife may be carrying a baby. If you have refrained from immoral act now, you will have undergone the best training and discipline for restraining yourself from immoral acts during your marriage.

Strange as it may sound initially, one of the best reasons for refraining from pre-marital sex is that it eliminates any chance you have of really getting to know who you want to marry. Once you start a sexual relationship that is all you and the would-be spouse will think about and plan for. You will plot scheme, maneuver, manipulate and otherwise move heaven and earth to find the time and place for a sexual rendezvous. What God's word does insist on is sexual intercourse in the relationship for which it was designed, marriage. Someone once said that intercourse is God's weeding present for married couples, to be unwrapped on the weeding night within the commitment of marriage.

Isn't strange that I need to have to say that? Strange, that a Christian has to defend sexuality as a God's-given thing? You open your Bible and you come to the Song of Solomon. There it is, an oriental love poem extolling the beauty of the beloved and the desirability of making love to such a wonderful person. It's there in the Bible Lush imagery, warm with passion, taut with unfulfilled desire.

So why is it in the Bible? Surely to show that the God who made human beings in his own image and planned that ' the two shall become one flesh' means it to be that way. How sad is it that Christian down the ages have wrapped it and twisted it until some of them have become ashamed even to think of their own or another's sexuality. It disturbs me to meet so many people for whom sex and spirituality are completely unrelated—or exist as opposites. For those who were brought up in a world where religious influence was nonexistent or plain ineffective, it may be a novel idea to consider that sex can be spiritual. Others, like me, grew up in a war between spirituality and sensuality. In my loving Baptist family, the word "sex" could stop conversations and make everyone freeze in embarrassment.

Implied Commandment about Sex Ethics

The first step in the spiritual life is to move beyond narcissism and self-absorption. This is not a glamorous suggestion, but it is essential: Treat your partner honestly, respectfully, and kindly. It's as simple as that. Spirituality begins in achieving a basic but difficult aspect of maturity—not being selfish. This doesn't mean that you don't take care of yourself and have full satisfaction in your sexual life, but, as the spiritual traditions consistently teach, love your neighbour as yourself.

Partnership

Sex is a union of persons, not only bodies. You can prepare for sex by being an interesting person, bringing with you your intelligence, culture, ideas, values, and talents. It's one thing to make love with a pretty body and another to be intimate with a real person. You can take time to talk to your partner, maybe at dinner before the act. Don't be afraid to talk about the things that matter. Letting a closely guarded thought emerge can lead to a physical sense of release. If you can't do this with your partner at dinner, then your sex may not be anything special

Vision

A spiritual person has a broad vision. He or she is interested in God, life, meaning, and the world. Vision is an aspect of transcendence and a reach beyond self. Sex usually begins and ends in conversation. Visionary talk, in contrast to mundane and self-centered chatter, can be vital and erotic.

Contemplation

Spirituality benefits from some kind of meditation in the word of God, a stepping outside the ordinary reality. Lovemaking can have a contemplative quality—taking time allowing yourself to dream God's mind on marriage, giving in not only to passion but also to the timeless intimacy of sex. "To stand outside," and it doesn't have to have the swoon factor that people sometimes associate with it. Ecstasy can be a steady, calm progress to a state that is tranquil and otherworldly.

Spirituality

Sex is as much a spiritual as anything done in church or worship centers. A spiritual is an action that speaks primarily about relationship with God and our reaction on the earth as his ambassadors. It doesn't have much practical meaning. Some people like to justify sex by seeing it as a way to make babies or to express love. Obviously it can do these things, but it can also be a means that evokes the spirituality of the relationship especially in marriage.

Generosity

Sex can be virtuous without being repressive or too clean. The great virtue in sex is generosity, the capacity to offer an abundance of feeling, intelligence, and equality to your spouse. This doesn't mean surrendering completely or giving away too much, but rather a thoughtful and moderate offering of self. Again, this is a traditional spiritual virtue applied to the special realm of sex.

Beauty

Sex has a lot to do with appreciating the beauty of the human body and the person. You don't have to be a stunner or even pretty or handsome. Fortunately, sexual passion allows us to see the beauty of the body in small elements and gestures. Loving the person also helps because the beauty of the personality usually gets transferred to the body.

Prayer

Prayer takes many forms. Even the monks have said that to work is to pray. You may or not say formal prayers before sex, but you can bring to it such an appreciation for its power to express love and to make unions that it becomes a prayer.

Community

Spirituality involves reaching beyond the self. Sex is quite private, but a good sex life can help make a good community. One of the results of good sex is joy of togetherness, pure and simple, an antidote to the often depressive, cynical tone of modern life, with its tendency to dehumanize and make excessive demands. When people have a joyful, positive outlook, they are capable of community.

The Two Extremes

Right:

So sex (in the sense of sexuality) is good, glorious and God-inspired. It is a part of my humanity, a great creative aspect of my being made-in-his-image and I will not debase it into a sordid, shameful, guilt-ridden desire, to be kept under and repressed.

But the world is not short of fools. Always manage to get things upside down. And the fools have really made a fine old mess of sex. On the other side are the Christian fools who come in two sizes. The first ruined sex by their fear of its power. There have let fear dominate them and there have even been extremists who have castrated themselves in the hope that such step would solve the problem.

Left:

But there is also the other kind of naïve Christian who forget that man was made in God's image. He is a child of what the bible calls the "Fall". Christian or no, we all have the capacity to taint what we touch. We aren't perfect. We are sinners even when forgiven; 'At one and the same time;' wrote Martin Luther, sinners and yet, justified. The Christians who can't believe himself or herself is capable of sin is in need of some hard study in John's first letter. And, if sin, then committing sin in the field of sex is just as possible as in any other areas of life.

Of course we mustn't forget the other sorts of fools. As the Psalmist wrote, 'The fools are said to himself; "there is no God"' (Psalms 14:1). In twentieth-century Africa there are plenty of fools like that whose lives admit of no creator, nor master and so, quite logically, of no restraints upon their behaviour. For them, sex is an appetite to be satisfied as and when they wish and with whom they wish. No Christian can possibly accept their view of life or their way of living it. It is as simple as this: I am a man under authority. I am not my own master. I have been bought for an unbelievable price, the life-blood of Jesus Christ.

Freedom to Choose Right

That means just this. I gladly accept that any sexuality is God-given. But I also sadly accept that my sexuality is a field ripe for self-exploitation. It's one aspect of my sinful nature. Only one. But it's still there and I dare not delude myself into forgetting it. It's not my sexuality that's shameful. It's me.

So I treat sex and all that goes with it with respect. Know it can be great as an experience. I know too that it can go wrong as an experience. But right or wrong, enjoyable or frustrating, as an experience is only one side of it. The other is the right or wrong of the actual motives and action in moral terms. For the whole sex and falling-in- love bit needs both to be right-the experience and the morality?

Christians therefore accept what they believe to be creative restraint upon their sexuality. They don't go to bed with people at the drop of a hat (nor should it be a skirt?). They don't treat each other's bodies as amusement arcades - mere fun palaces. They know the way that their chemistry works and the powerful instincts which a bit of the old slap-and –tickle arouses. They are cautious about rushing into wild embrace simply because it's enjoyable. In other words, Christian believes in marriage or to use the language of sociologist, in permanent pair-bonding. They see the union of two bodies sexually as the symbol of a total commitment - 'the two become one flesh' to which they add' under one master-God.' And they keep sexual intercourse within that relationship.

Watch Out

Get that foundation principle clear and you're on the right road to sorting out the practical questions which face every young unmarried boy or girl.

So what are the practical questions? Let's take them in the logical order; First question: Are there any limitations on which I should go out with?

Answer: If God is my master then I cannot contemplate a relationship with someone who refuses to accept his Lordship. That's not a petty restriction. It's an obvious part of my discipleship. And suppose I experience 'falling in love' with an unbeliever. Does that make it right? No, certainly not. After all, if I 'fall in love' with someone who's already married, it doesn't make adultery right.' Falling in love is not a self-validating experience. Lots of people are very prone to 'falling in love.' But my emotions along are no sure guide to what is a right course of action. My feeling may be like of yo-yo. Only a fool lets his feelings, his moods and his emotions, become master of his actions.

Second question: How far can I go?

Answer: As Eric Morecambe would say,' there is no answer to that.' But there are useful pointers. Try asking yourself whether you are doing whatever you're doing because you like it or because it is a genuinely appropriate action at the state which your total relationship has reached. In short, that it ought to be a mile-stone at the end of a part of your inter-personal journey, not the sign post at the beginning. I've tried to spell all this out in my book, Key to a happy marriage, why not read that?

Last question: Must every friendship be started with one eye on the possibility of the wedding ring or altar consummation?

Answer: Of course not. Men and Women can and should learn to be good friends as Christians. But it doesn't take long to realize that once the touching starts it's better to be open with each other and sort things out or someone is sure to get hurt. Good friends don't have to be lovers (even in terms of the most minimal intimacies) but they do need to know just where it stands. That is only fair. Kisses do have a way of being misinterpreted.

Underlying it all is prayer. 'Lord' please guide me and keep me from making a fool of myself or from hurting anyone else. Please show me the way which is your way and give me courage to take it.' That kind of prayer gets answered.

When I am writing this to myself I said, 'It's impossible to do justice to it in a few hundred words.' So it is. That is why you read more in the book 'Keys to a happy marriage. May be you will have a taste for the book. In the meantime put God first and thank him for your sexuality. Then ask him to help you to use it responsibly. That's what it's all about.

Marriage And Divorce

Many Churches observer believe that the Evangelical/Pentecostal churches are more and more, suffering from the fall-out of the free and easy sex revolution of the 70s-80s had spring to this millennial. The sad fact is the many of the most sincere Christians even in position of leadership, have been strongly influence by this trends over the past 20 years there has been a wholesome erosion of Biblical attitudes towards adultery and divorce.

Praise God, it is not as awful in Nigeria or some part of Africa as it is in Britain, America and other part of Europe, where divorce is our epidemic in the Evangelical and Pentecostal Christian community. I was shocked when I went for further studies in United Kingdom years ago and discovered that many top Christian speakers, gospel singers and preachers, quietly slip off to the divorce court to shake their spouse while continue to preach and minister without any check in momentum and nobody seems to in the least of bothered.

Though the Nigeria church has not quite shipped into Britain habits of calling adultery "an affair" and offering 'quick' divorce on demand, the winning signs are everywhere in Nigeria churches. But we must face the fact that more and more Christians are conforming to the world in respect of their attitude to adultery and divorce. So our main concern must be to find what scripture says.

God's Answer God has expressed himself very bluntly on both divorce and remarriage. On the first of these he puts it in three word,' I hate divorce.' On the second he says whoever divorces husband or wife and remarries 'commits adultery.' See Malachi 2:16' Mark 10:11, 12.

If this sounds sweeping, remember that the way we are made is already pointing in this direction, since we hardly need the Bible to tell us that men and women are not things to be scrapped as soon as they cease to please ('Trade in your husband/wife for this year's model') and the fact that the sexes are-in more ways than one-a match for each other suggests that a married couple will need time and patience to achieve anything like a mature relationship. It is also well known that the children of marriage depends on their parents too long and too deeply to come out unhurt from a domestic break-up-particularly as their very dependence tends to make them a centre of dispute, the rope in the parental tug-of-war.

But the Bible takes all this much further by showing that we exist for God, stamped with his likeness. It follows that much more is at stake than one's private or even shared convenience and happiness: What God wishes becomes the first and last question on the subject.

Old Testament Order

God's design for marriage is laid down at the outset of the Bible (Genesis 2:18-25). Moreover Jesus appeared to this pattern as basic for all time. It shows the first man and woman as divinely-planed companions, each the compliment of the other (for the famous expression's help meet' means just this). The whole interest of the story of Eve's creation is in this personal partnership and in case we should miss the point, a line is drawn straight from Eden to every marriage in the words "Therefore shall a man…cleave unto his wife and they shall be one fresh. 'These are the words Jesus quoted.

So the first and final sayings of the Old Testament on the marriage bond reinforce one another and both are based on the concept of partnership.'… she is your companion, 'says God through Malachi, 'and your wife by covenant. 'Yet he middle pages have a deferent look, for divorce was taken for granted in the law of Moses, and at one time of crisis it was even commanded, in order to undo a tangle of foreign marriages which was choking the Jewish community of Ezra's day. So it is hardly surprising that the legal experts whom we meet in the Gospels were debating not whether divorce was allowable, but only what made it so.

New Testament Order

Jesus, has ever, pierced straight to the essentials. To him the law was not a set of regulations to be studied for loopholes, but the voice of God about practical truth and love. Inthe Sermon on the Mount (Matthews 5:27-32) before he mentioned divorce he spoke of adultery, and in both cases he made us look at the realities of our behaviour, not the legal niceties- for we may be comfortable within the law in our acts and right outside it in our thoughts; or unassailable on our rights and damnable in our relationships.

But in Matthews 19 he went further still. He pointed out that marriage involves you and your creator. It is his work you pull apart when you get a divorce. Jesus put it unforgettably, in a phrase the Marriage Service has borrowed for its moment of climax: 'What…God has joined together, let no man put asunder' (Matthews19:6). So the whole trust of his teaching is toward the level at which you are shamed out of tempering with so high a matter, and divorce appears as an outrage against man and God.

The Only Exception

Yet the Old Testament had provided for divorce and remarriage, even while it spoke against it. And Jesus defended this on the simple ground that men must be governed and laws must be workable. In fact he went further, for he made one exception himself to his absolute prohibition, puncturing it buy the clause 'excerpt for un-chastity', reported twice by Matthews5:32, 19:9. So the New Testament like the Old seems to speak with two voices. What are we to make of it?

Certainly we must make no more of it than the New Testament does. The exception is almost invisible: Mark and Luke give no hint of it, and Matthews in reporting it makes it clear that it did nothing to lessen the disciples' shock at the high standard Jesus was setting. If that is the position, the exclaimed, it is better to refrain from marriage. It was the principle that had registered with them, not the exception.

Second, Jesus confined this exception to the one sin, un-chastity, which touches the unique relation of Husband and wife. Other sins can destroy companionship and make separation advisable – always in hope for reconciliation (Paul provides exactly this in 1 Cor.

7:10 – 11) but only un-chastity can strike at the marriage state itself. So the unique exception highlights the unique relation: it says, as strongly as the rest of the teaching that one's partner is not for sharing.

Third, Jesus saw in the Old Testament divorce law the truth about man, not about marriage. 'The creation story shows what marriage is; the divorce law only what mankind has become. The same can be said of Jesus' own teachings: the very fact that unchastely has to be mentioned in the same breath as marriage proves that 'the hardness of your hearts' is nothing obsolete. If it must be provided for, that is our shame, not our right. Finally, the whole force of Gods example, as well as his words, is towards an unswerving fidelity. God's people, his bride, may have deserved divorce a thousand times; they have had his reclaiming love instead. This is why, exemption or no exception the Christian church sees divorce and remarriage as virtually unthinkable, a contradiction (in all but a tiny minority of cases) of the love which 'bears all things, believers all things, hopes all things, and endures all things.' This is the love we have reactive; this is what, on our infinitely smaller scale, we must give.

What Is The Church Saying About Contraceptives?

We can conveniently consider this by asking five further questions on specific points. In the beginning

We're not Adam (Genesis 1:28) and Noah (Genesis 9:1) instructed to be fruitful and multiply the earth?

Yes, but they were on an empty planet. Since then the earth has been replenished to such an irresponsible degree that the most frightening problem facing it is not atomic weaponry but the population explosion.

The divine command the continued 'and subdue it.' Nature is to subdued. God said to Eve, 'I will greatly multiply...thy conception' (Genesis 3:16). The Hebrew allows us to take this at it face value. Hyper-fertility may indeed be one of the curses of the fall which we can legitimately tackle as we have tackled the companion curse of weeds by our agricultural methods and of painful labour with our analgesic techniques.

Today when tens of millions of children in Africa and other part of the third world are starving it is increasingly obvious that to be pro-life may demand being anti-birth. In these underdeveloped lands today it is often true that to permit an addition to the family is to pronounce a death-sentence on the present youngest child.

Rationale of Marriage

Solomon tells that 'Songs are a heritage from the Lord, and children are a reward from him. Happy is the man who has his quiver full of them' (Psalms 127:3-5). Should we not accept as many children as God send?

Marriage was ordained by God for the mutual companionship of man and woman. We are told three times, 'Therefore shall a man leave his father and his mother and shall cleave to his wife and they shall be one flesh.' Walter Trobisch comments that on each occasion the text end with a full stop: there is no mention of children (I married you). While the blessing of children is stressed repeatedly in scripture, their production is not the chief end of marriage. That primary purpose is impossible, in the view of many people, if children arrive in annual succession.

Rosemary Reuther, a Roman Catholic, has written. We come to the ironic fact that in our present situation man is only able fully to say "yes" to procreation if he is also to say "no" (Contraception and Holiness: the Catholic Predicament) For in almost every marriage however much the parents love children, there comes a time when the wife knows that her recourses of time, of strength, of emotional response, of money, will not stretch to provide adequately for another child. No doubt if one arrived they would get by, but she is aware that that at best this could be achieved only by some deprivation in affection and care. Knowing this she can act responsibly only by avoiding conception. In the past this could be achieved only by encasing herself in an amour of emotional unresponsiveness. In other words she was in a dilemma: she either had to deny her union with her husband in one flesh, or her role as mother. Today however she has the option of continuing her close relationship with her husband, and at the same time of fulfilling her call to be homemaker, by employing contraception.

Working Against God's Purpose

As some God's messengers have been aware that he choose them before birth (Isaiah 49:1, Jeremiah 1:5, Galatians 1:15), may we not unwittingly frustrate God's plans by preventing conception?

First we have to realize that God must overrule even when conception is planned. It is not widely known that that the production of the male sperm is so vast that at any one normal act of intercourse there are about two hundred million different possibilities as to the genetic character of the baby to be initiated. Sperm competition is such that the child conceived at 9 o'clock is different from that which would have been conceived twenty minutes earlier. Once conceived there is a great, perhaps even 50% chance that the pregnancy will not precede successful, most of this loses occurring so early that the woman never realize that the egg had been fertilized. If despite all this, God is able, as we believe, to achieve his purposes we do not need to fear that our decision will upset his plans. By the same token, abstinence from intercourse, whether in marriage or by celibacy, powerfully limits God's freedom of action.

Results with the Lord

Is it right to use artificial means? Why not practice normal intercourse and leave the results to the Lord?

This sounds very spiritual. There are few however who advocate such reliance when it comes to other spheres of life. We wear safety belts, we take out insurance policies, Those ofus who are parents ensure that our child's milk supply is bacteria free, that the family have an artificially purified water supply, that if they are liable to infection they are artificially supplied with artificial protection in the form of inoculation or vaccination or prophylaxis. If we are ill, we take appropriate drug. The population problem arises today because we have practiced death-control. Were we wrong? Should we allow four out of five of our children to succumb to disease in their first mouth, or should we protect them by every artificial means at our disposal-and thank God who has made there means available?

It should be noted that God withdrew his miraculous supply of manna as soon as the Israelites were in a position to look to their own food supplies.

To Be Sterilized or Not

Sterilization surgically produced contraception which should be considered as virtually irreversible. Where there is a medical reason why the married woman should not have any more children it would appear to be a wise step. Also if there is a strong possibility of an abnormal child resulting from a genetic anomaly in ether parent, that parent may consider sterilization.

Problems arise in people's minds as to whether they should be sterilized when they feel they have completed their family. In a situation where all other methods of contraception have been tried and have failed, there is a clear case for sterilization. However, many Christians have opted for sterilization even when other methods were available to them. In our judgment each couple must decide together what is right for them, but we would strongly advise against the operation if either partner has any reservations.

Perhaps the most powerful argument in favour of the use of a trusted contraceptive technique is that in our clinical experience we have found that any other course leads to tensions and frustration in the marriage, tension which spill over adversely to affect the children. It is irrelevant to consider what mighty has been the course to which God called his servant in a different age. He has placed us in an age where contraceptives are available, where child survival has been artificially and beneficially manipulated by science. It is in such an age that we have been called to manifest his life, and to accept his provision with thankfulness.

Views On Abortion

Let us first be clear what is meant by abortion and what it involves. Abortion is the ending of a pregnancy before its 28th week; it is only beyond this stage of development that a child born alive is considered capable of a separate successful existence. A modern medicine however has enable babies born even four weeks early to survive. In future years furtheradvances mighty be made and the child of such an early birth may well be able to continue to adult life. So there is no fixed stage of development beyond which a child born alive will be able to survive, and inevitable fail to do so if born earlier.

The Child in the Womb

'Legal' abortion is usually done in the 13th to 18th week of pregnancy, or even a little later. The legally aborted child, had it been born alive spontaneously instead of being deliberately destroyed, could under appropriate conditions have survived for a little time. With improved paediatric techniques the child at the stage of development may, in years to come, also be able to survive even to manhood.

At the time when most legal abortions are carried out the child in the womb has all obvious essentials for continuing existence. It moves, react to painful stimuli, it heart beats, it urinates, and in appearance is a complete miniature human child. Though lying in the womb, it is no part of the mother, and has its own independent blood system. Since conception it has been a separate individual, genetically deferent from either parent, and in fact it is entirely parasitic on its mother, absolving its requirements from her blood simply through placenta.

Thus abortion, the killing of a small live separate individual human being, whether done within the law or in the secret, is murder before birth, just as much as it would be murder if the child were destroyed after birth.

The Christian View

Human life for Christians is the on-going process of our creation by God. It is sinful to take human life, so for a Christian human abortion is also as sinful. The respect for human life shown by a Christian should include removal of anything endangering life; it is as culpable passively to let human life be destroyed, as it is actively to destroy it.

When a pregnancy imperils the mother's life, there is the dilemma of balancing the life of the mother against that of her unborn child. To remove the child at a stage when it could not survive-that is by abortion-inevitably means killing the child. Some Christian would leave the solution to God; but many other Christians would consider that, being endowed with intelligence and free will, it would be reasonable for them to protect the mother's life, if she wishes, by aborting the pregnancy.

Another problem arises when it is known that the child will be born abnormal. Some Christians would consider this justification for abortion, there by compassionately sparing the mother the burden of bearing and bringing up such a child. But an abnormal child in a family need not be a tragedy; there are many examples of such children uniting members of their family in Christian compassion, to give them happy lives. It should also be remembered thatserious, permanent, handicapping abnormality can strike any member of a family, child or otherwise, as the results of illness or accident, and there can be no questions of murder them. Many Christians would not consider abnormality of the unborn child as justification for abortion. But there can be gross abnormality in an unborn child that would rob it of individual existence, for example the anencephalic without brain. Most Christians would accept abortion in such a case.

Thus many Christians would justify abortion in those instances where the mother's life seems to be imperilled by the pregnancy, or her health, physical and mental, appears in danger of serous permanent damage, or the unborn child is likely to be born very seriously abnormal. But such abortion is nevertheless sinful. To same Christians it seems justifiable; but not so to others.

Other Thoughts

Arguments have been advanced for abortion in a verity of other circumstances which aggregate to a plea for abortion on demand.

First, the unwanted: It can happen that the unwanted pregnancy does not lead to an unwanted child, when it arrives. On the contrary, such a baby is often well loved. But this is not always so and we must aware of the hardships which sometimes face such a child.

In the case of the lone mother, certain social and economic considerations arise. Illegitimacy is no longer a social stigma. Many women whether married or not bring up their children alone, but not nearly enough is done to help these women with their practical difficulties. Society has a duty to help solve their problems, but not to liquidate them. Single women with children can and do marry happily, as do the widows and the divorced.

Whether a child is made to feel unwanted depends on the personality of the mother, married or single. It is her responsibility. Unwanted pregnancy in itself is no justification for abortion.

Second, in the name of woman's rights: Next are the abortions labeled as women's rights? It is claimed sensibly that every woman has the right to control her fertility; but such a failures is one of the risks which has to accepted in sexual relations, and leads on to the unwanted pregnancy-a social matter, not a case for abortion. It is also said that every woman has a right to decide what she will do with her body. It is also said that every woman has the right to decide what she will do with her body. If is true for any person, it still does not give a woman the right to destroy the living body of another individual, the child she helped to put into her womb. Another version is that if it is permissible to remove an offending part of the body, such as a troublesome appendix, tooth or tonsil; the same should apply to a pregnancy. But this is not valid comparison, as the unborn child is no part of the mother's body, but is the separate body. One strange theory is that a doctor who does not agree to abort a pregnancy is forcing the mother to carry the child to full term against her will. Every doctor must be free to act according to his conscience. It is the patient who has put herself in the position of having to carry the pregnancy.

When abortion is considered, there is often reference to the rights of the individual and to Christian compassion. The unborn child has the right to go on living, and is worthy of Christian compassion.

One should not try to judge people. Those directly concerned in an abortion, if they are Christians, are making their decision before God; he is the only judge. Those who have no faith cannot be measured by Christian standards. Likewise those who are not directly concerned in an abortion decision should not judge those who are. They cannot know the full and real circumstances. Should they be directly involved one day, they may find that their preconceived ideas slip under stress.

It is said by some that it is unfair that it is the woman who is left holding the baby. Motherhood is to the vast majority of women a privilege they would not give up, even if they did not give up, even if they did not come to it readily in the first place.

A Gynaecologist's View About Abortion

In modern life, circumstances and problems arise about which the Bible does not seem to give specific guidance: but general principles are given, which can be applied prayerfully to every situation. Abortion is such one problem, involving theological, moral, legal and physical issues, and causing much distress to individual and families. Whenever emotive factors influence decisions, the Christian can only hope to make right decisions by adhering to biblical principles.

The Worth of Human Life

What value does God place in the human life? High enough to create a world of beauty of men to live in, and to give his son, Jesus Christ, to save him! Psalms 139 shows that God is concerned about the development of the foetus (vers13-16; 'Thou didst knit together in my mother's womb… my frames was not hidden from thee when I was made from secret. Thy eyes beheld my unformed substance…') and the sixth commandment states that 'Thou shall not kill' (Exodus 20-13) Therefore, should deliberate termination of foetal life ever beperformed? The Romans Catholic Church says' no,' not ever in the rare circumstances when the mother's life is endangered.

The Chronological Backdrop

Historically, the aim of the Medicine has always been to preserve life, and we know that in Greco-Romans times, i.e. pr-Christians, abortion was sometimes practiced, but the physical taking a Hippocratic Oath (c.400BC) swore not to do so. In England this standard applied throughout the Middle Age and in 1861, the Office against the Person Act stated that it was a felony to procure, or attempt to procure, an unlawful abortion, and a convicted person was liable to be sentenced to penal servitude for life, with or without hard labour. In 1929, the Infant Life Preservation Act stated that 'child destruction' of a foetus after 28 weeks was a felony equivalent to murder or manslaughter, unless done in good faith for the purpose only of preserving the life of the mother.

Does the timing of when the foetus receives its soul (or rather, spirit) help one to decide whether abortion in the very early stages can be acceptable or not? The Bible is silent on this point, but I have found it helpful as the consultant said practice to think of the value of the individual to God and likewise of the potential individual, whether he receives his soul at conception or latter. If one says at conception, there is the problem of the many thousands of spontaneous, extremely early abortions when the foetus is still incompletely formed, but if one says later there is difficulty in fixing the exact time: is it the moment of viability (which varies with advances of medical science and their availability) or not until birth, when the foetus becomes an independent individual? I feel that this dilemma does not detract from the main principle of respect for life and potential life and abortion is rarely justified except in the presence of grave maternal illness, either physical or mental and should not be done for trivial reasons or used as a form of contraception.

Abortion is but one aspect of life in a permissive society and the Christian should make every effort to be an influence for good in society. With regard to the individual needing help, Christ's principle of compassion should be paramount, but tempered with his command 'Go and do not sin again' (John 8:11) Where applicable.

Homosexual Christianity

There are few subjects that arouse such violent and emotional reactions as homosexuality. And as with most discussions of this kind, the homosexuality debate tends to generate more heat than light. Those of both sides of the argument are sometimes guilty of misunderstanding the facts, and the confusion that results is to nobody's advantage. It will be helpful, then, to begin with one or two important distinctions.

Some Clarification

Perversion

The pervert is a man or woman who is basically heterosexual in orientation, but dabbles in homosexual behaviour for variety, curiosity or kicks. Inverts, by contrast, are people who have never known what it is to be attracted to members of the opposite sex. For them homosexual attraction seems perfectly natural. Many observers, bracket all homosexuality with perversion. That is unfair and confusing. The vast majority of all homosexuals are inverts, and their members are significant possibly as high as one in twenty-five of the total population.

Gender Is Determined At Birth

Sex is something determined at birth, it is anatomically obvious to midwife and mother whether a new-born baby is a boy or a girl. Gender on the other hand, is a far more complex matter. It has to do with feelings, attitudes, tastes and character.

Encouraged by the media, Hollywood or Nollywood and especially by the advertisers, we tend to distinguish sharply between an approach to life which is essentially masculine and a list of character-traits and attitudes with are labeled feminine. Unfortunately, not all those who have the genital apparatus of one sex fall into the 'right' side of the gender divide. Some 'men' find themselves trapped in female bodies, and vice versa. It could well be well that many people feel themselves to be inverting homosexual when what they really mean is that they fail to share the feelings and characteristics of their sex, as set out in the glossy periodicals.

Conduct

By no means has all inverted practice as homosexuals. Many try to suppress their feelings. Some get married and have children in the desperate attempt to appear 'normal' in a world that is still hostile to homosexuality. When we talk about accepting homosexuality, we have to distinguish between those who feel that way, and those who act on their feelings.

Friendship

This is the vital distinction which is difficult to draw. A kiss, an embrace or even a handshake may be the prelude to sex-union or a mark of friendship, depending on the circumstances and the attitudes of those who give and receive the gesture. It is important to distinguish homosexual behaviour from physical expression of friendship which is wholesome and right.

At this point social pressures may influence our attitudes more strongly than we think. Englishmen are not surprised when they see two girlfriends exchange a kiss in the street, butthey are horrified if they notice two boys doing the same. On the other side, in Africa you seldom see people embraced in the street. Our differences of social outlook must be taken into the account if our moral judgments are not to be clouded.

Immorality

This point follows closely on the last. It is all too easy for us to label things we find distasteful as immoral. But not everything that nauseates us is morally wrong. The sight of the man eating raw eggs may make me sick. But he has not acted immorality just because I do not like what he does.

This is a distinction we must be particularly careful to draw when we judge behaviour between two people of the same sex. Most homosexuals find the very thought of homosexual conduct disturbing if not disgusting- but that alone does not make it immoral.

Lasting union

It is always a mistake to dismiss other people's opinions by caricaturing them. Homosexual behaviour is often bracketed promiscuity and condemned for much the same reasons. The change sometimes sticks because lasting homosexual union seems particularly difficult to achieve. But it would be quite wrong to assume that all homosexuals only seek partners for occasional physical gratification. Many sincerely and desire a resting bond in which sex plays a minor role. We may still believe that such a life is wrong, but we must be careful not to condemn it in the same breath as we decry a one-night stand with a prostitute.

It is wrong

Distinctions of this kind underlie the insistent appears we hear we hear today for a more liberal approach to homosexuality. If same people are so made that they can only form intimate relationship with a number of their own sex, why should they be denied something the homosexual majorities freely enjoy? Modern scientific knowledge has helped us to understand the invert homosexual. Now is the time, we are told, to convert understanding into acceptance by revising our civil and moral law-codes, to allow homosexual to fulfill themselves in the only way they know how.

On both sides of the Atlantic prominent priests, churchmen echo these sentiments Jesus, they remind us, summed up all moral values under the heading of love. How, then, can it be wrong for two people who care for one another genuinely, and who intend to stand by one another for life, to express their affection through the physical channels God has given them?

Biblical View

Jesus used his Bible to unpack the true meaning of love, and we must do the same. At no time did he hint that a loving motive could make a wrong thing right. It is important therefore to sift out the Bible's teaching on homosexuality in order to find out whether a 'gay' relationship can ever be acceptable in God's sight.

Wherever the Bible mentions homosexuality, it bans it. What is not always so clear, however, is whether all homosexual relationships came under the biblical veto.

The Sodom incident, for example (Genesis 19, Judges 19:14-28) demonstrates the extremely serious view God takes of all homosexual assault- but it says nothing about the rightness or wrongness of a tender homosexual relationship where there is full consent on both sides. The law of Moses goes further by condemning homosexual behaviour alongside adultery and incest (either of which may involve a love-bond), but it uses the word (Abomination) which is normal reserved for idolatry (Leviticus 18:22, 20:13). In other words, God's judgment on assaults and idolatry is clear. But does he also condemn a homosexual relationship where there is no attempt by one partner to force his (or her) favours on the other, and no desire to worship false gods?

Some find these doubts reflection in the New Testament's teachings. Paul is very blunt in outlawing homosexual in his letters to the church at Corinth (1 Corinthians 6:9) and to young Timothy in Ephesus (1 Timothy 1:10). He also condemns, in the strongest language, those who have 'exchange natural relations for un-natural' (Romans 1:26). But do his stern words apply to the invert as well as the pervert? The invert homosexual may well feel he has no such 'natural' relations to exchange.

The doctrinal foundations on which Paul builds his teaching sweep all such doubts and hesitations aside. In Romans, his verdict on homosexuality is based on God's creation plan for man and woman. By 'natural relation' he means natural to man and woman as God created them' and homosexuality played no part in the creator's scheme. In 1st Timothy, the condemnation of practicing homosexuals is built into Paul's own updated version of the Ten Commandments; and more commandments, as we know, reflect the main principles of creation as they are outlined for us in Genesis. It comes as no surprise to find that in 1

Corinthians the veto on homosexual conduct occurs in a list of behaviour-pattern which finds no place in God's kingdom where the Creator's will is perfectly done.

The conclusion is unmistakable. Deeper foundations could hardly be laid for biblical teaching on any subject. Modern distinctions, important though they are, are undercut. The New Testament puts an emphatic ban on all homosexual behaviour.

We Must Make A Separation

There seems no reasonable doubt that homosexual conduct must be clearly labelled as sin. But the Bible distinguishes sharply between sin and the sinner. Everyone has weaknessesof some sort, and homosexual tendencies are not to be put in same special class of their own. As sinners we need the support from other Christians and homosexual need this supportive fellowship more than most because loneliness is their worst enemy. Some fear that the danger of ostracism, if they own up their feelings in a Christian fellowship, is too great a risk to run. Where this is true, the church bears a large measure of blame.

God accept us as we are, and his church can hardly do less. But God also seeks to change us, and again the homosexual is no exception to the rule. Some Christian's homosexuals find that whole sexual orientation undergoes a radical change when they open their lives to God's power. Others have to fight the same old temptations, in God's strength, all their lives. But, as many hetero-sexual men and women have found, the single life is not a second-best if it is part of the God's will. Jesus himself lived a perfectly fulfilled human life even though he never married.

Is There Anything Wrong With Pornography?

Are there any moral questions, as opposed to moral certitudes attending the subject of pornography? At first sight it would all seem so clear. By definition, lexicographical or legal, pornography expresses or suggests the obscene; and the 'obscene,' again by definition, is offensive to modesty or decency, moral question which arise about pornography once it has been identified as such would seem of the different order from those which appear when we are trying to pinpoint whether certain writings or pictures can be categories as pornographic.

Hence there are two clusters of questions: about pornography. One cluster has to do with identifying it. The other has to do with the nature of the 'offence' to which, if present, it gives rise. The clusters are closely related, but the difference between them is as important as their similarity.

Identification of Pornography

To take the first cluster of questions: how do we, indeed can we identify pornography? The problem here is that, even by dictionary definition, absolutely and relative scales are both applicable. To be pornographic, the writing or painting must suggest the obscene and the obscene is offensive either, to modesty or decency' or' to the senses or mind, 'or both. This is where the strongly subjective element in the whole discussion became so important. We must begin by facing the fact that as individuals we do have different levels of tolerance, whether it is to pain or pollution: that the air on which some thrives is death to the consumptive: and that the same is true of moral pollution. Hence what affect the senses mind of one may not affect the sense of mind of another. But there is a level of our pollution beyond which no known human being can survive; and so miners and soldiers have died. Secular society is slowly discovering that laws which operate in the physical realm to operate similarly on other dimensions of living, and that the spirit of a man can be shocked as surely as his body. Hence the obscenity laws society promulgates in its own defense. But there is no basic of agreement about where to put the safety limit; though we now have agreed measurements of sound levels destructive to humanity or environmental pollution levels inimical to well-being, society has not yet really agreed on a similar Plimsoll line indicating that which is dangerous to the senses or mind in the realm of the obscene.

The reason for this is perfectly clear. There is going to be little possibility of harmonizing the relative measurements when there is no agreement about the absolute. To say of something that it offends 'modesty' or decency' is, today, to beg the question about whether such qualities either exist or should exist; and that in spite of the goodwill which may felt, in a vague and spongy way, towards both. To be pornographic means in some way to damage or violate human value; and if the humanity concern does not of itself recognize that it has been damaged or violated, that its modesty or decency has been assaulted, it is extremely tricky to prove to it the case. It is difficult to restore to a burglar's victim property which he swears he never lost in the first place.

It will be apparent from this that the identification of pornography has to do with one's view of the nature of man and as such as the moral dimension shaped by what our understanding is of his origin and destiny. If we believe man is God's creation, shaped in his maker's image, created to share in the divine delight, then our understanding of his essential activities and functions will accord with this. Mind and senses, modesty and decency, would then be offended by anything which denied either the delight or the sacredness of the sexual relationship: anything which divorced it from the real situation of the person, so that it led him away from a God - directed reality into a state fantasy; anything which perverted the sexual by rooting in the sadistic or the masochistic instead of the giving and receiving of delight.

Questions We Must Ask Ourselves

So there are certain questions we must ask ourselves strictly if we suspect writing or painting of pornography. There are few better tests of either our honesty or our humility than the way we face the questions.

First, does this work suggest the creativity and self-giving which properly attend a sexual relationship, or does it deny them? Why does it do so? Is it because one's own nation of sexual freedom and dignity is too rigid and narrow, or because this expression of the sexual is debasing?Secondly, does this work stimulate me to a sexual excitement which is not correlated with my circumstances, so that I am led to a fantasy life which denies my real situation? (This is not to deny the importance of fantasy in life but to assert the need for it to be recognized for what it is, rather than a substitute-reality which becomes pretence for the real thing) More fundamentally, does it present a view which illuminates and depends or denies the realities of the sexual relationship? Does it depend for its effect on glamorizing and removing the mundane responsibility of the sexual, or at the other extreme, on its operation, or on the abnormal?

Thirdly, does it present sexual relationship in terms of self-gratification and the 'using' of another, merging into the abuse both of the other and of oneself? That is, are the roots of it presented implicitly or explicitly, as violence and hate rather than love?

It is surprising how hard it is to answer these questions entirely honestly. Obviously we are all hostages of our society to some extent and we have to face seriously the current claim that pornography can to the some degree be therapeutic. It is at this point that the divergence between the Christian ethic and the current social ethic becomes most apparent. There are two questions here. First, how far any of us can so detach himself from the society in which he lives that his values are not completely modified by it. C.S. Lewis has said much on the way we became insensibly adjusted to the mores of our society, so that, unaware, our code of discrimination is changed. Secondly there is the question of how far the Christian has any right, as a member of a minority group, to prescribe for society laws which related to his faith, the foundation for which are to be found in the Christian view of man (Romans 1:18-32, Colossians 1:15-19, Ephesians 4:17, 5:33).

There is no space here to expand the approach to these questions, beyond two essential points. In relation to the first, the Christian is called to live in two worlds throughout his life, in the society of the day and in the community of the body of Christ. If he fully live in both then there is an inbuilt system of counter-balance which will prevent him from ever becoming wholly assimilated to what Traherne has called 'the dirty devices of the world' while he yet remains sensitive to what society may have to teach him (which last in its check on false pieties, pharisaical smugness, lack of insight, and self-generated sectarian view, can be very valuable). In relation to the second issue, since the Christians, is declaring not what he thinks to be good only for Christians, but what he feels to be a fundamental truth about the creature man, the claim that Christians should not apply their views beyond their own minority group is irrelevant, just as environmentalists are concerned with what affect man whether he admits it or not, so are Christians, and there is nothing overbearing about their saying so.

A Plagued Society

This leads us into the second cluster of questions, those arising from the nature of the 'offence' to which pornography, once identified, gives rise. For the gap between What a Christian identify as pornography and what his society may so define says something about the society itself. Here the close relationship between the two clusters of questions becomes obvious, and also the difference. The first cluster had at its centre what the Christian view is of man. The second cluster retains that view, but goes on to put at the centre of the question what it is that reveals itself by the presence of pornography. For the truth is that pornography itself is a symptom, not a disease; it is a significant eruption by which the nature and extent of a society's ill can be diagnosed. Where it exists to any significant extent it indicates society which regards people as object, not as being of infinite worth which has lost the capacity of reverence towards its individual members as creatures of dignity and sacredness; which is tormented and rends itself in violence, hatred and self-abuse, and which abandons responsibility in the context of realities for a dream of power and achievement in a fantasy world.

The question which arise here are twofold. What should our attitude be towards a society so revealed? And secondly, what can or ought to be done about it? Again space allows for only the briefest approach. Concerning the question of the Christians attitude, the key to his proper understanding must be that he is himself member of the society he so diagnoses, and must stand under his own judgment. The self-righteous, minatory, merely accusatory, denies the truth of this, and was never a posture Christ himself adopted. Rather he came to the sick and searched out the cause of the sickness. Such 'searching' does not indulge the sickness that is astringent, does not compound with, but removes the root of, the disease.

It is important that Christians should be prepared to confess to themselves, as well as publicity, those ills of which as members of the society they stand convicted. There can be no gap between public and private here. It is a measure of our society's double-think that it can urge such a distinction and suggest that what is experienced in private is not a matter of concern for anyone else that only a public pornography is of importance. As John Donne said, 'Any man's death diminishes me, whether it be physical, moral or spiritual. So the distinction between public and private stances seems to neither be a non-question, nor can one make the issue one of 'harm' to others only, since by definition pornography is harmful.

What Can We Do?

This brings us to the final question, which can only be broached after we have looked at all the foregoing. The last question is the one usually raised first, hence the ambiguities and misunderstandings that arise. The concluding question must be: 'what is to done about pornography?' And here there is properly a twofold approach, on private and the other public. The private approach involves a humble and honest self-scrutiny which test both one's self- righteousness' and one's own self-indulgence in the context of one's living relationship with God and one's fellow man, and adjust one's practice accordingly. The public approach will require so positive expression of the real glory of the human beings proper state that the way pornography represents him will be seen by comparison as diminishing and derogatory. Such an expression is to be made not only in words but in deeds and relationships and its quality is essentially joyous, not denunciatory. It is true that nothing so dispels the effect of pornography as laughter. But there are different kind of laughter, and that which most quickly not only heals the offence but also create new life is the joyful laughter of the humans being who delights in his Creator and in all things he has made.

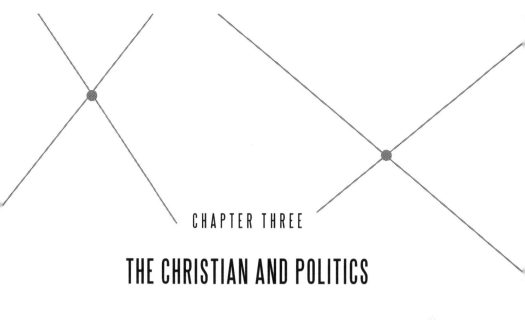

CHAPTER THREE

THE CHRISTIAN AND POLITICS

All over the globe today, societal values are being redefined by its political cultures and religion beliefs. This will be the subject focus of this third chapter. We need to provide right answers to questions being raised by critical minds in respect to modern society, politics and the roles of the Christian.

The Ideal for Society

The ideal of free Society needs further pondering and deeper postulations. Since one of the fundamental values of western democracy is that of freedom of speech, the idea of any sort of official control of the spoken or written words, or of what is visually conveyed by pictures or acting naturally starts with the presumption that it is to be deplored. Censorship is an emotive word. A censor originally meant quite simply a person who reckons or estimates the value of something. But now, primarily, censorship has come to be used of the control of human communications. It is particularly applied to the control of what may be said in public, publishing in printed form, or represented pictorially or upon a stage.

However, everyone in most civilized and democratic societies knows certain restraints upon communications have always been accepted as being for the wider good of that society. Thus in our own country what may be discussed publicly about certain aspects of Government policy is subject to the official act. The inviolability of legal proceedings once they have been commenced is protected by the law of contempt Blasphemy is restrained by certain legal sanctions.

Let me digress slight on this subject about the hypocrisy of the Western governments who are quick to preach good governance to Africa but they fail to preach the same message to their banks who act as safe havens for these corrupt leaders. The western governments have forgotten that the existence of bank secrecy laws in Switzerland, Jersey Island, Britain, Liechtenstein, Luxemburg, Austria have encouraged these corrupt leaders to bank away monies meant for their countries' development.

The name of Switzerland, Britain, France, Jersey Island, Liechtenstein and Luxemburg came up several times throughout this study of corruption in Africa as I try to establish where most of the stolen monies go. Even though these countries like to portray themselves as civilized and cultured with hearts of angels, they have failed to recognize that keeping monies that were dishonestly obtained from the poor people on earth taint whatever reputation they might have. In the case of Switzerland and her allies who keep these stolen monies it is so pathetic that they know they are receiving stolen monies yet due to greed they have done nothing to stop it.

The next time you are looking for stolen money from your country ask the Swiss government and the Swiss banks they always have a clue about it where about.

Africa is poor today because of colluding and connivance of Swiss and other western banks and the kleptocrats who rule Africa. Corruption is rife on the continent because those who steal the money never lack a place to hide them.

Fighting corruption should not be left to the poor countries alone. Western media who always portray Africa as underdeveloped and backward must expose the banks in their countries who serve as safe havens. The media should put pressure on politicians in Europe and America to reform the banking secrecy laws and make it punishable offence to receive monies from these corrupt leaders. Again the western media must campaign vigorously for all looted monies to be returned to their rightful owners in Africa. The western media must team up with civil organizations to expose western companies who pay bribes to secure contracts in Africa like Acres International, Halliburton, Trafigura, Achair Partners and Progresso.

Western countries have a duty to stop their nations being used as safe havens for stolen monies from the African continent. Western countries should reform their banking laws. They should return all looted money put there by corrupt African leaders to the African people. There must be an international coalition dedicated to tracking all stolen monies on the face of the earth with Africa given to priority.

Africans must demand transparency and accountability in government. Laws must be enacted in Africa to protect whistle blowers who take the risk to expose corrupt practices.

While it is very important to sympathize with the presumption in favour of freedom as a useful starting-point, will must never forget that man is by nature sinful and has tremendous potential for exploiting his neighbour. Aggression and corruption are in his heart from birth as well as the instinct to seek nobler things. It is there for both realistic and biblical to watch for those types of communication which are peculiarly harmful and infections, and to restrain them in any age.

Censorship

How much official control is needed will vary according to the moral quality of the cultural context? It is now time to look in a little more detail at the various type of control which might be included under the heading of censorship. Professor peter G. Richards in parliament and Conscience (Allen & Unwin) provide a useful four-fold analysis:

Censorship may be formal informal, it may be prospective or retroactive. Formal censorship depends on rules of conduct imposed by authority while informal regulation stems from social taboos. Prospective censorship operates on materials before it is publicly available so that the censor's decision may not became public knowledge, while retroactive censorship suppresses matter already published pre-publication control is more effective and convenient for a censor because the alternatives invites widespread comment on his decision.

Retroactive: Formal and Informal

Following the four-fold division given above, let us first consider retroactive censorship i.e. that which affects a publication's status after it has appeared and been made available. Formal retroactive censorship is simply the matter of law. The rules are existing registration and those who apply them are the courts. A man publishes but at his own risk. If his publication is unlawful, it is suppressed in the sense that he is punished and the offending article whether statement or pictorial matter no longer circulates. In a democracy these decisions are only taken after a public procedure which ensures that competent people determine whether or not the law has been broken.

Informal retroactive censorship signifies same kind of tacit agreement that certain things shall not be accessible to the public even though the law does not prohibit them and there are those willing to make them available. Such a reaction is exemplified by people in the distribution chairs on through which article are conveyed to the public, such as film distributors and exhibitors, and the newsagents' distribution chain. The decision not to stock or to distribute a book or a film can effectively secure its suppression.

Prospective

Informal prospective censorship has been and still is typified by the activities of the broadcasting media. Within radio and television, in both the commercial and the public service bureaucracies, individual men and women are invested great power of informal control over broadcast material. This has always been so, but it is a fact of life which many in our society have not yet faced. In the days when honest people are in charge of media, this control was largely exercised in such a manner as to respect what might be loosely called Christian moral standards. Material challenging such standards or offensive to them was not broadcasting by the tacit agreement of all the personal involved. In the same way censorship (if we may call it) is now exercise in precisely the reverse direction, so that strongly Christian statement and viewpoints are rarely expressed, and same radio and TV broadcasts already reported are never transmitted because of their clear moral stance. This informal pre- censorship applies also to certain organization replicating particular viewpoints, who cannot get articles or letters into the correspondence columns of certain newspapers,; and when the commercial interests which support the independence broadcasting Authority channels are also those who have large or controlling holding in mass circulation newspapers the possibilities for censorship are even more sinister.

Informal prospective censorship can be seen therefore as something which may from a Christian point of view be good or bad. When it is exercises in the sphere of moral to keep the tone of public discussion responsible, sensitive and respective of human dignity, then offensive and degrading materials will rarely appear by tacit consent. However in the sphere of political discussion and information it is vital that there should be adequate treatment of all view point and possibilities, and in particular that no commercial interest should wield power over communications which they may exercise to the moral detriment of the community, this we conclude that Christians will be very sensitive to commercial or political manipulation through informal prospective censorship, but grateful for those informal arrangements which exert a controlling moral filter in this area.

Our final variety of censorship is formal prospective censorship. The most precise usage of the word and probably the one for which it should retrained. In this sense we speak of the close body (however appointed) which screens or sifts material according to known criteria before such material may publicly communicated. Formal prospective censorship is widely used in totalitarian countries where any information likely to raise doubts in the mind of public about the wisdom of the policies adopted by the dictator or the only political party permitted to exist is not granted public expression. Because of its close association with tyrannical forms of government, formal prospective censorship is deplored and usually rightly so.

Film Censorship

An early screening process by a responsible public body is not always a bad thing, even in a democratic society. The main requirements must surely be that the powers of such a body must be clear and its criteria and decisions open to public scrutiny. Properly applied, such powers can serve those wishing to publish offensive material from the risk of prosecution and from wasting resources on a particular enterprise by consulting the censorship body beforehand.

The board of film censors in Nollywood is not a statutory body and their certificates have no legal value. The fact that it has refused to grant a certificate to a film cannot prevent it exhibition. Local authorities' possess' power by which they can refuse to permit the showing of any film, or they can alter the classification of any film from that on the certificate which the board has awarded. Few local authorities welcome the task of maintaining a viewing committee which regularly previews questionable film on behalf of local community standards, but in response to public protest many have rightly comes to accept this as part of their own duty on behalf of the health of the community. They deserve the sympathy and support of all Christian citizens.

Where public taste is good, pure and strong, there is little need of censorship even the law will not be needed often. But where the moral consensus is weak, where perverted individuals and commercial interests are heedless of social damage or even trying to wreck society and its fundamental institutions such as the family, a strong law at least will be needed and perhaps even pre-censorship too. Montesquieu said 'Where religion is strong the law can be weak, but where the religion is weak the law must be strong'.

The Church And Politics

Is It A Directive From God That The Church Should Be Silent On Political Affairs? The answer to this question depends entirely on what you think of politics. What is politics?

'Politics,' says Ambrose Bierce in his Devil's dictionary, 'it is strife of interest masquerading as a contest of principle the conduct of politic affairs for private advantage.' But what is the Devil's definition. As Tokunbo Adeyemo (2009:80) asserted in his book "IsAfrica Cursed" The words 'politics' and 'political' comes from the same Greek root as the words "citizen" and "citizenship. Polities, which means citizen refers to a member of a city or state or inhabitant of a country or district, or simply a citizen.

Broadly speaking, 'politics' denotes the life of the city, polis and the responsibilities of the citizen, "polities". Therefore, politics encompasses the entire aspect of life in human society.

In the context of such a broad understanding, John Stott (1984:11) defines "politics" as "The art of living in a community". But in a narrow sense, politics is "the science of government", which develops and adopts specific policies as enshrined in the constitution and the laws of the land – and as government inevitably has profound consequences for those who are governed, it is unthinkable that the churches voice should not be head in the political arena. When we think of politics in the narrower definition of it, otherwise we are all "politician" or citizen in the broader sense of the word.

Tentatively, we can say that in one sense or the other, Christians cannot evade politics although there are some Christians who think they can. Yet this is an illusion because whether you live in a monastery or a jingle, this is a political world. Instead, the question we should ask is "how" and not "whether" a Christian should be involved in politics.

The prophets of the Old Testament certainly made their voices heard. They talked vociferously about the vices of the King and the greed of the landowners, about inflation and international treaties, about injustice and luxury. Amos, for example came to the regarded as political agitator and a menace to the establishment. Jeremiah was imprisoned because he spoke against the war. The prophets took up their unenviable task at the command of God because they were concerned about the effects of government upon the common man. It was their way of loving God and loving their neighbour.

Given the facts then that the voice of the church ought to be heard in the political arena, how is it to be heard? Should Bishops speak to law makers, Clergy to write to the members of the house of Parliament State and Federal, and Christian academics to contribute to the correspondence columns in national papers? What exactly can be done? I suggest three possibilities.

The Christian Witness

First, individual Christian, who might be listening for a call to the ordained ministry or to the mission field, or to the social services or to the medicine, should be alert to the possibility of another calling, ie the science of government or politics. The prophets were for the large part of ordinary men/women called of God to influence the decisions which their rulers were making and to summon the nation to the bar of God's judgment. They were not spectacularly successful at the time, but their utterances live on as a constant challenge to rulers and politicians and government officials.

The church's voice, if it is to be heard at all from within the political arena rather than from outside it. The spectator may see more of the game but he has scarcely any capacity for influencing the results. The committed Marxist is often to be found in the places of maximum power and influence. He has no need to raise his voice in public. He may be just an under- secretary or the head of department or a newspaper's correspondent for political affairs or the convener of his union branch. Good luck to him – he deserve his success. But it would be a pity if the Christian case, which is often a thoroughly practical and persuasive one, should go by default for lack of anyone to sustain it.

The Church Community

Second, the local church should take the science of government seriously and accepts its responsibility at local and national level. There are many practicing Christians in both Houses of assembly, many more in local government and in union management. They need to feel the ground-swell of support from the church; they need more help than they commonly get from the congregation to which they belong.

I seldom hear prayers in many churches for the local officials by name. What about the members of house assembly who may be involved in a crucial debate the following week or for the local councilor who has to chair an important meeting on certain burning issues or for the chairperson at the local government as he/she struggles with some bitter dispute? They need to be remembered personally. There are some parishes big enough and flourishing enough to constitute themselves into 'support group' who would make it their business, not only to pray but to know and to act.

The Church and the Nation

Then the church as a whole should attend with greater seriousness to public affairs. There are more people than we sometimes imagine who are calling to the Church to do just that. For the past thirty or more years, for reasons good or for reasons bad, the church in Nigeria and in most countries in Africa has been steadily withdrawing from public life. The time has come to arrest drift. The time has come to try to articulate in political terms the kind of Christian aspirations to which many millions of our countrymen/women still give silent assent.

Too often, we simply react to pressures from outside or protest at decisions already made. We trail rather limply in the wake of enthusiastic that unbalanced minority movements or climb on to bandwagons at just the point where they are grinding to a halt. This is no way for the Church of God to handle its responsibilities to the nation. We enjoy marvelous resources of knowledge, expertise and devotion in the church, but no apparent means of mobilizing them in the interest of a clear and practical approach to the great issues which trouble us all. The leaders of the church have some responsibility for being also leaders of the nation.

'Ah,' you will say,' the church may never agree about anything. How can we achieve a Christian consensus in politics? No consensus is necessary. It is only necessary that Christians should have been expose to the realities of the political situation and are thus able to react to them in the light of their own conscience, added, I trust, by the mind of the Church as it has been exhibited down the centuries. We are not looking for a Christian political party; subject to the whips, voting one way, huddling together, but for Christian in every party of every persuasion who will act and try to cause others to act against the background of God's prevailing will for mankind. We need men and women who are as devoted to God's kingdom as they are to this nation Nigeria and Africa continent.

'Render to Caesar the things that are Caesar's and to God the things that are God's,' Jesus said. We have not begun to penetrate to the meaning of those enigmatic words, but at least they suggest that there are duties to Caesar and there are duties to God. The duties to Caesar are as arduous as the duties to God and seldom prove to be singularly frustrating.

Politics is the art of the possible and compromise to inseparable from it. Solid results depend on the willingness to accept certain conventions and certain inescapable condition. The author of Ecclesiastes tells how 'there was a little city and a few men within it; and there came a great king against it and besieged it, and built great bulwarks against it. Now there was found in it a poor wise man, and he by his wisdom delivered the city. Yet no man remembered that same poor man' (Ecclesiastes 9:14-15). No matter – he did deliver the city.

The Christian in public affairs may not make a name for himself. He may get precious little thanks. But by the gift of divine wisdom he may be enabled to deliver the city.

Does Christianity Have Anything To Do With Politics?

There are many Christians who believe most strongly that a Christian should not get mixed up with politics. They believe that politics is a dirty game and that Christians should have no part of it. Yet there are other Christians who feel exactly the opposite. They believe that Christians in responsible positions can do great good and that political power should not be allowed to be a monopoly of those who might abuse it. Which of this two is right?

People in Power The Christians starts from the belief that, as Paul taught, 'the powers that be are ordained of God' (Romans 13:1). This was also taught by Peter (Peter2:13-17), and by our Lord in his famous saying, 'Render to Caesar the things that are Caesar, and to God the things that are God's (Mark 12:17). In the context, the expression 'the powers that be' refers to government and the primary purpose of government is to maintain order, to restrain and punish evil and to reward good.

To do this, governments do not have to be perfect. Governments in the days of Christ and the apostles were imperial and arbitrary, not nationalist or democratic. Their governors were unjust and took bribes, and their tax collectors took more than their due. But the Christians were told by Christ and the apostles to obey them unless they interfered in matters of faith. If Christians were forbidden by government to preach the gospel or told to worship the emperor, then, of course, they disobeyed. As Peter said, 'We ought to obey God rather than men' (Act5:29).

In most countries in the world the Christian has about as much chance of becoming a part of government as Peter had of replacing Pontius Pilate or Paul had replacing Festus or Felix. Their duty of obedience to the lawful commands is the limits of the Christian involvement in politics. In countries where the ruling party is atheistic or committed to another religion, the Christian cannot be a member and is effectively excluded from politics and power. He may still, like Joseph and Daniel, act as an adviser, but he will not allow himself to be committed to the belief or shibboleths of the ruling party.

Christian and His Circle of Influence

Yet we have to remember that the influence of Christian outside politics can still be enormous. It was the Christian Church which survived and not the Roman Empire, and Christian ideals which were gradually accepted through Europe rather than the ideal of the Romans. Even where Christians have no place in politics, they can by their ideals and examples gradually change the political climate in which they live. We are taught to pray for rulers and those in authority. We are also taught to pray that God's will should be done on earth has it is in heaven. We should believe that God can answer the prayers he has taught us. But Christ also taught that' whoever takes the sword shall perish with the sword' (Matthew 26:52). It is not only lack of faith but disobedience to attempt a violent overthrow of government, even a corrupt and arbitrary government like that of Imperial Rome, Europe and elsewhere in Africa.

In most countries where Christians influence has prevailed there are democratic governments and a Christian can stand as the candidate for election to local or national government. Many Christians feel that they have no right to impose Christian principles on those who are not Christian. They also feel that it would be wrong to compromise those principles for something else. So they feel that they cannot accept political responsibility. Their problem is that they do not distinguish between the moral law under which man answers to God and the civil law under which we answer to our fellow men.

The Moral Code

When Christ said that divorcé was contrary to God's will it was pointed out to him that Moses allowed it-and who was he to contradict Moses? His answer was that Moses had allowed divorce for the hardness of their hearts, 'but from the beginning it was not so' (Matthews 19:8). Moses was the civil order. He gave Israel the Ten Commandments, which embody the moral law. But he also gave laws of the land-rules for the people of Israel to be enforced by their rulers. If a man love his wife as he love himself, according to the moral law he will not divorce her. But hard-hearted men, though they cannot be persuaded to keep the moral law, still may be persuaded by the penalties of the civil law not to throw out their wife without going through a proper form of divorce in which the law will protect the wife's rights.

A Christian politician who passes bills allowing divorce does not deny his principles any more than Moses denied his. Both are doing their best in the circumstances. But a Christian politician can also try to persuade his-fellow citizens to raise their standards. Wilberforce and his friends abolish the slave trade. Shaftesbury and his friends preventing the abuse of child labour. Both groups acted as Christian politician on Christian principles.

All countries need some ultimate moral standard. No country can survive for long unless there is a moral basis to its laws, a basis of which men can agree. Those who are not Christian try to make up their moral basis. But why should anyone agree with them? They tell people not to be greedy and no one take too much notice. It's needs more than exhortation to turn back greed, to curb violence, to make the rich pay taxes to help the poor, to make the strong stand aside to help the weak. The Christian in politics can contribute his knowledge of the divinely revealed moral order which men are happier if they keep and which has been applied and tried in all kinds of societies for two thousand years.

But politics is also about power, and power, like money, can corrupt. The Christian in politics must not regard power as his supreme objective. In his attempt to be elected and to gain power for his party he must do nothing against the Christian standards of conduct. If he does, he will destroy his usefulness as the Christian. The saying; 'If God be for us who can be against us?' is not a guarantee that Christians will win election without trying? But Christians have found that a reputation for honourable behaviour does not in the end hinder and, after help them, to get elected.

Trade Unionism

The question presupposes that the Christian is a member of his union. For some it is not as simple as that. The first question may well be, Can I Christian belong to the trade union? Will it spoil my witness, my separateness? Some would quote the words of St Paul,' Do not be mismatched with unbelievers;' and, 'Therefore come out from them and be separate from them, says the Lord, and touch nothing unclean' (Corinthians 6:14-17) Read in this way the passage mighty seem to suggest that we should opt out of any organization, profession, clubs etc. to which non-Christian belong. But if the passenger is carefully studied alongside such a story as the parable of the Good Samaritan (Luke 10:29-37) and the teaching of Jesus abut salt and light in Matthew 5:13-16. I believe it will be seen that the general tenor of scripture is on involvement, not on separation. Separation depends on a close walk with the Lord, not on external conditions

The Involvement

To be of any use in anything we must be involved. The chap on the touchline may spur the centre-forward on, but he can't score the goal. If he is watching the match on TV in his front he is even less use. A Christian trade unionist must be prepared to get involved. Paying ones dues is not enough. Salt is the only useful if it is doing his job of flavouring and purifying.

Not everyone can become general secretary of his union, any more than every redeemites can be an overseer. But in a union as in a church there is a minimum requirement for a faithful member.

If I can continue the analogy, the early Christians were told not to neglect to meet together, as was the habit of some (Hebrews 10:25). Today the same thing might well be said to trade unionists. One of our major weaknesses is the poor support given to branch meetings; shop floor meetings and district meetings. One even reads of strikes which involves thousands of people being continued because only hundreds have turned up to vote whether to return to work or not. Needless to say that those who do turn up are the so-called militant minority usually comrades? Yet the Christians are called to be militant! Paul sees the Christians life as a battle and the Christian also as a soldier. We find him using the army as an example again and again.

Christian certainly ought to attend their union meetings. This is not, I hasten to say, in order to oppose any party or sector (the Christian may well find themselves voting and working with them on same issues) but to bring God's justice into the situation. The Bible has much say about wages and conditions, employee/employer relationship, safety at work, work itself and attitude to it. Get hold of a good concordance and search out the truth of this. Ezekiel 37 will make a fair start.

Position

We have differing gift, and just as in a church situation same are called to hold office others are not, so it is in the unions. I fear however that Christian are often afflicted with deafness when the Lord calls them to serve in trade unions. If you are ask to stand for office, make it a habit of prayer and ask your church and your Christian friends to pray for wisdom to be given to you. One of the great things about our faith is that we don't have to agree with what a person is doing before we can pray for him in the doing of it. If you do accept office as a branch secretary, money steward or shop steward, you will need that prayer support, so keep people informed when you have important meeting or are faced with big decisions. You will also need to recognize that this sort of work will limit the time you can devote to the more conventional Christians spheres and activities.

In favour say 'yes'

Even if holding office is not for you, voting most certainly is. Most union official are elected by a small minority of the membership. Far-reaching decisions are often arrived at by a handful of members. So your vote is important. That means knowing what it's all about. Only too often at meeting I notice people looking round to see how those 'in the know' are voting before raising their hand. Equally I have quite often find myself voting for or against an issue and being a minority of one-only to be approached afterwards by someone who said, 'I agree with you, Johnson, but what's the point when you're so out-numbered?

If you have got an opinion, you ought to have the guts to show it. To have an opinion will mean discussing with others, reading union journals, broadsheets and newspapers, listening to radio and television debates, and picking out what is said by and about various candidates. Yes, it takes time, it means work, and sometimes it's boring. And yet I believe it is all parts of loving one's neighbour as oneself.

Your Own Support

Recently I spoke to the clerk of Lusaka council about the fact that after making a great display of strength on a particular issue, their council executive settled for a very small part of their claim. 'Well' he said,' Expect they looked over my shoulder for an army and found it had deserted. It was true. What they were asking for had little support from the rank and file. Members had no stomach for the fight, and the leader knew it. I need hardly say that there are limits to backing our leadership. The apostle were quite firm with the early Christians that they must obey all lawful authority because it is ordained of God. In many countries including ours trade unions are a lawful authority, protected by parliament or statute and the courts. Yet when Peter and John were ordered by the lawful Jewish authority (the rulers of the people and the elders) not to speak or teach in the name of Jesus, they flatly refused to obey them (Acts 4:19-20). So our final authority is God. We may at some point have to stand against our leadership if its decisions are clearly contrary to God's laws. This is something which could only be done after much thought and prayer. It could be costly in terms of employment, friendship and even health. We follow one who said it should be so. It was for him.

Must We Always To Obey Those In Authority?

'Authority,' like 'love' is a much misused word. People tend to make it mean what they want, it to mean. Before we can consider whether we should always obey those in authority, therefore, we need to be clear about what we mean by authority.

My working definition is this; authority is power exercise legitimately.

As you will later see, such authority stems from belief, belief in the right of a person giving an order or instruction to be obeyed or followed. This means that 'authority' and 'compulsion' do not really belong together. A bully is not exercising authority when he compels a smaller and a weaker to do what he wants, but is forcing his will upon another person through the exercise of what may be called 'necked power'. Authority, on the other hand, involves the recognition by certain people that another person has the right to exercise power. This means that we can go a long way towards answering our question, should we always obey those in authority?' By asking another, 'Have they the right to demand what they are asking?'

Authority Exercise Legitimately

The view that authority is power exercised legitimately can be illustrated by the attitude of the public at large to certain groups within it, such as the police, teachers and the government officials. Much of the prestige of the police, for example, depends upon the recognition by society that when a policeman is on duty he has the right to expect co- operation and obedience. A police man is not obeyed simply because of the sanctions he may use against us if we disobey, but rather because we believe he has the right to expect us to obey him.

In recent years there have been come serious crises in authority. Demonstrators have refused to obey police, students have refused to conform to school rules and section of thepublic has tried to ignore the authority of the state. Some, disturbed by this growing disrespect for 'the authority' (as they sometimes call them), may then over-react by demanding that authority be imposed by mean of stronger sanctions against those who disobey. In the sense in which I am using the word, however, authority cannot be imposed, it has to be accepted and where disbelief in a person's right to exercise power in present, real authority is absent.

This view of authority finds support in the New Testament, for the Greek Word exousia usually translated 'authority' carries with it the idea of power being exercise legitimately. Jesus talks about having the right (exousia) to lay down his life and to take it again (John 10:18), and demonstrates that he has a right (exousia) to forgive sins by healing the paralytic (Matthews 9:6-8). Paul claimed the right (exousia) to marry and to expect financial support from the church he was serving (1 Corinthians 9:4) and clearly believed that God has authority over people just as the potter had authority (exousia) over his clay (Romans 9:21).

Against this brief New Testament background, we can begin to see how Christians ought to answer the question, 'Should we always obey those in authority?

The Source of Authority

First, it can be seen quite clearly that ultimate authority rest with God, for as Creator and Redeemer he is Sovereign Lord over all. We owe him complete obedience. But how can we know what God want in order that we may obey him?

The answer is clearly related to the Christian belief that Christianity is the revealed religion, which means, in short, that God has not left us to grope our way toward him but has taken the trouble to reveal himself and his will to us. God has revealed himself uniquely in the person of Jesus Christ, the Incarnate Word and all that we need to know of God-revealed-in-Christ is contained in the Bible, the written word. We know God's will by listening to Jesus; we hear Jesus by reading the Bible.

What this means in practical terms for everyday Christian living and not least for an answer to our original question, is that the Bible is the norm, the yardstick against which our beliefs and practices have to be measured. So what does the Bible say about whether we should obey those in authority?

The Bible makes it clear that there is a direct conflict between the known will of God and some human demand and admonishes that God's will should be done. So for example, Daniel was right to refuse the imperial edict forbidding him to pray to God (Daniel 6), and Peter and John were right to refuse the Jewish Sanhedrin's order to give up preaching about the resurrection (Acts 4: 19). On both occasions, believers choose to obey God rather than men. It would not be difficult to find similar modern example. But it must be remembered that the choice may be the costly one.

Other institutions

After allowing this overriding principle that obedience to God takes precedence over obedience to any human being or institution, the Bible sets out the general rule that Christians they should obey those who legitimately exercising power over them. In the nation, for example, Christians are commanded to obey government (Romans 13:1-6) in such practical matter as keeping the laws and paying taxes, for, says Paul, 'the authorities are in God's service.' In a democracy, Christians have the added incentive of knowing that they can help to create a more just (and therefore more Christians) society by the way they use their vote and exercise their influence.

Paul, like Moses before him, also has something to say about where authority lies in family life, for after making the general point, 'Be subject to one another out for reverence for Christ' (Ephesians 5: 21), he went on to say, Wives be subject to your Husbands as to the Lord' (v 22), 'Husbands, love your wives, as Christ also loves the church' (v 25), and 'children, obey your parents'(Ephesians 6:1).

The same writer proceeded to deal with relationship 'slaves' and 'earthly masters,' and although under the influence of the gospel slavery was eventually abolished, the principles Paul sets out in (Ephesians 6:5) will repay study and are capable of being applied to same extent to the relationship between the employers and employee.

Should we always obey those in authority? The Biblical answer seems very clear. Yes, provided that what they demand is not in direct conflict with what God demands. But this does not mean that the Christian must not try to get to 'authority' (national, managerial, church, parental or any other) to change their minds or modify their demands, if this should seem to be necessary in the interest of truth and justice.

Is It True That The Church In The West Have Accepted The Guilty Of Imposition Of Cultures?

The Burden of White Man

Taking time to scan through some popular missionary literature of the Victorian era will force as to admit that this has frequently been the case. Especially during the colonial era, this coincided with the modern missionary movement, western civilization was inseparable intertwined with the Gospel so that some countries within 'Christians' tended to regard themselves almost as God's gift to the universe. It was naively thought that their material prosperity was the result of God's special blessing; a reward for their piety. Along with the Gospel was offered the European and North American cultural heritage, which represented in the eyes of the missionary the outworking of the Gospel. As a consequence, national cultural tended to be discounted or undervalued. There were, however, notable exception among the missionary ranks, and in all our criticism we must remember that the missionaries despite their shortcoming were more sensitive than their fellow countrymen, who were motivated by commercial interests.

The Peril of Today

If we now need, with the perspective of history, to correct the triumphalism and idealism which marked the missionary movement until the First World War had its humbling effect, we also need to guard against today current of cynicism, which regards the missionary movement as a huge con-trick designed to sanction and support the west's colonial expansion. To write off all missions in these terms is to fly in the face of the evidence. The missionary movement was not the result of the church management policy decisions to initiate an export drive. It was carried out in the face of apathy and open hostility of the ecclesiastical establishment. In addition, not a few colonial administrators regarded missionaries as a danger to themselves and a disturbing influence in their territory, and did all in their power to obstruct missionary endeavors.

In the development of mission mistakes galore have been made, some of them with tragic consequences. The same can be said about the development of medicine, alongside the errors there have been many remarkable achievement. The missionary movement has established Christian Church around the world, so that today there are far more Christian outside the old boundaries of 'Christendom' than within it. If missionary expansion had been dependent upon colonial influence, we would have expected the church to fold up with the assumption of independence. In fact quite the reverse happened-the growing edge of

Christianity increasingly to be found outside Europe and North America. In some instances the Church is flourishing despite a hostile environment. Additionally, we must not forget that it was the missionary movements which introduced and manned and trained national personal for the medical and educational services which the newly-impendent nations have rightly taken over.

Today there is a far greater sensitivity to culture values in non-western civilization.

Many missionaries, trained in anthropology and sociology, are seeking to interpret the Gospel in local cultural settings. National Christians and their missionary colleagues are sensitive to detect areas in which western Christians have distorted the Gospel through additions, subtraction and division.

More to the Gospel

Western Christians have added to the Gospel attitudes of mind and patterns of behaviour which they have made part of the package. Their attitudes to work, their stress on economic self-sufficiency and their regards for possessions have bred materialistic attitudes. In some areas, mission has been promoted with the technique dependence characteristics of big business. For instance Latin America's Evangelism-in-Depth programmed has come in for the great deal of criticism on account of its dependence on success-guaranteed methods, high- powered missionary technocrats, and stereotyped massage content. Latin American protest has led to an entirely new approach, with nationals determining the programme so that it is appropriate for a given areas.

In some countries becoming a Christian almost entails becoming a ' foreigner' in the eyes of the people, as they see the convert beginning to express himself in Western thought forms, dress differently (in India preferring the suit to a dhoti or a dress for a sari), and use unfamiliar forms of music. The devotional content of church services is still largely dependent of North America and European piety. An electric or pipe organ may be installed in church as a mark of prestige even though such instruments are virtually unknown in the country at large.

Something to Remove

Western missionary have tended to stress the individual and private aspects of religion to the detriment of the corporate and community emphases of the culture in which they work. They have also been blinkered with the regard to the socio-political dimension of the Gospel, so that Latin American theologians, evangelical as well as liberal. Accuse them of preaching a truncated and inadequate gospel. In their social aid programmed, the westerners have in the past concentrated on the alleviation of symptoms, rather than investigations and exposing the cause of poverty, disease and ignorance. Also, their stress on the theoretical and the abstract has suppressed the emotional and non-rational dimensions of true communion with God and encounter with fellow believers.

There Should Not Be Any Division

Though their highly individualistic evangelical approach and stress on the need for personal decision for Christ. Missionaries from Europe and North America have sometimes caused needless divisions within families, and alienated individual families from their village communities. Such division may result from the differences the gospel makes, but in some instances much conflict could have been avoided by the more sensitive and patient approach. In certain culture the decision will be a family step rather than an individual one, and in village life a people's movement may occur. Anyone coming to another society needs to be sensitive to the cultural as well as the theological obstacles to faith.

A further serious aspect is the way that Protestant missions have divided the body of Christ into umpteen denominations. There are over 250 in Nigeria and in many countries around the world you will find Northern and southern Baptists. Which has nothing to do with their location in the country, for instance, the split in the Baptist ranks was caused by American Civil War. Why should this be carried to Africa?

Let Us Work On Unity

Yet there are many encouraging signs that David is throwing off the cumbersome Western amour. National Church unity schemes, third-World understanding of the gospel, worship enriched by local culture, new patterns of ministry and spontaneous growth all provided clear evidence of life.

The Church overseas are also doing the service to the Church in the west by reminding Christian there of dimensions of the gospel which they have conveniently forgotten and by rescuing them from their uncritical local attitude. The presence of such people in the west will provide some much colour to the 'White man's religion,' so that it will become less of a mirror reflecting the attitude of Western society and more of a light bringing the challenge of the gospel of the kingdom of God.

What Is the Justification for Violence?

The Christian is called to love his neighbour. This love is to be expressed in a deep concern both for man's spirituals need in everyday life. The difficulty lies in keeping these two aspects of ministry in balance together. Evangelical and Pentecostal Christians have sometimes tended so to emphasis the evangelistic call that the social side of the gospel has been underplayed. Over the past decades the World Council of Churches and World Evangelical Fellowship has moved strongly in the other direction. At first this was expected in a concern for social aid, but it was increasingly realize that poverty and material needs, were often due to political structures which perpetuated injustice. Changing these political or social structures became therefore the new dimension Christian ministry.

Men of influence and wealth prefer to mention the status quo. Violence seems to be the only effective way to change the existing political system of operation in the search for equality and justice. So the WCC supports the revolutionary movement in Africa, and leading churchmen may be involved in violent activity in Latin America.

'Violent of same sort is inevitable', they say. 'Imperialism, economic oppression and social injustice are types of violence which leads to imprisonment, starvation and death. 'Isovert revolution perhaps a lesser form which may introduce a new society of justice and righteousness? This would be the view of many today, including the exponents of Black Theology and the Theology of Liberation. Other maintains that violence always breeds more violence and bitterness can never be the harbinger of love.

As biblical Christians we need to ask ourselves whether violence can be countenanced by Scripture. Mere philosophical pragmatic answers cannot suffice.

The Old Testament

The historical books

A strong emphasis on justice in everyday social dealings marked the life of Israel. Jehovah concerned himself deeply with details of life such as the right use of landmarks. Widows, Orphans, aliens and the weak generally where to be protected through an incorrupt judiciary. So Exodus describes Moses acting as judge over Israel. Then in chapter 18 he establishes a more effective system. This chapter teaches three basic concepts:

1. God is the supreme Judge over his people – and the Laws are his.
2. God's appointed leaders are to teach his ways of justice and administer them.
3. Corruption in the judiciary is uttered abhorrent to God.

In Deuteronomy 17 we find similar teaching with regard to the establishment of the monarchy. God allows Israel to have a king over them; he does not insist on a democratic form of government. But Israel king is to have certain characteristics: i. He is to be God's choice (17:15) and subject to God's law (17:18-19). ii. He must be humble because he is one with his people (17:15-20). iii. He will not trust in material wealth and power (17:16-17). iv. He is to be morally upright (17:17)

But this chapter gives no hint how Israel should deal with a bad king. The tacit assumption is that God will remove him. (17:20) Even the parallel passage in 1 Samuel 8 also teaches that it is God who chooses kings. The people can only 'cry out' if a king is evil; but still God does not necessarily answer their cry because of their sin.

The historical books do however reveal a God who is often violent and who sometimes commands his people to display violence. After the deliverance of Israel from Egypt, Jehovah is called 'a man of war' (Exodus 15:3). The distraction of the Canaanite race by Israel at God's command is also hardly pacific. The old Hebrew Rabbis explained this (Mechilta 38b) by saying that 'it is only for the love of Israel that God appears in such a capacity'. Others say that bloodshed is only for the distraction of pacific corrupt people in order to keep Israel from compromising relationship. God was teaching Israel the meaning of holiness. We cannot however avoid the fact that Jehovah and his people killed and destroyed. The Prophets

So from the beginning of Israel history, violence is common and the early prophets also do not avoid words which do not encourage such action, but they themselves do not indulge in the shedding of blood – e.g. Ahijah in 1 Kings 11 and Elisha in 1 Kings 19. The writing prophets however do not even incite to violent action. They merely preach impassioned demands for justice and righteousness, denouncing leaders who betray their high calling. The prophets are not activist revolutionaries. They believe in a God who controls history and will in due time establish his kingdom of justice.

The New Testament

Professor Brandon has tried to show that Jesus was a zealot revolutionary. Yoder, Hengel and others have shown this idea to be biblically indefensible. Jesus did not take arms, nor did he incite his disciples to join the rebels. He refused to be made a human king, insisting that his kingdom was not of this world. Finally he submitted silent to his judges and executioners, like a sheep before its shearers. Willingly and without resistance he suffered and died.

Many Christians today are calling the Church to resume a prophetic ministry in fearless preaching against all oppression by light-wing or left-wing regimes. Verkuyl also encourages Christians to use non-violent weapons such as strikes. But the prophet who is not prepared to resort to the ultimate extreme of violence will be rejected by both wings of political opinion. He will be also condemned by the revolutionary as being too passive and therefore favouring the status quo. Non- violent prophetic teaching will be rejected, and can only lead to the Cross. Jesus too was rejected by zealots as being too passive, while the Romans crucified him as a political threat. The servant cannot be greater than his mater.

However, the teachings of Jesus Christ undermined the authoritarian claims of the Romans. Thus for example Roman coin had upon them the image of the emperor and could therefore be given to him in taxation. Man on the other hand is made in the image of God and can only be subject to God.

In Luke 3, John the Baptist attacked inequality, greed and the wrong use of power. Jesus too in his miracles and in his teaching demonstrated his support for the weak and despised society. He did not hesitate to criticize the leaders of political and religious life. In his aggressive ethics of love, Jesus boldly attacked anything that savoured of injustice and hypocrisy. His words and deeds were socially revolutionary, but violence was not his chosen means to usher in the revolution. The apostles were accused of turning the world upside down. They caused disturbances in place after place by their words. The revolutionary power however was supplied by the Holy Spirit who was present in their prayer and teaching. They did not use force. They taught that as far as possible Christians should live peaceably with all (Romans 12:18)

The book of Revelation shows God in violence action of judgment and to the lesser degree we see this same divine violence in other parts of the New Testament. Its teaching is consistent with that of the Old Testament: such violence is the province of God and not of man. Man preaches and teaches the demand of God for justice and righteousness; but such zeal must also be tempered with patient realism which recognizes that the characteristics of the perfect kingdom of God cannot in this age be fully realized. On the other hand we are not to sit back idly and bemoan the world's slide into increasing evil as the climax of Christ second coming approaches. God's passions for righteousness and for social justice are to enflame our hearts and drive us to loving action in words and deeds. Nevertheless violence remains the activity of God in judgment

What Defense Can We Put Up For Capital Punishment

This question should really start further back. Is any punishment defensible? For punishment, properly speaking is an act of retribution and this word has few supporters now. We may feel that it should be replaces by the concept of reform, or at most, the protection of society and the deterring of other wrongdoers.

Retribution

But retribution deserves a closer look. For a start, God's own judgment is retributive. In a famous sentence, 'he will render to every man according to his works' (Romans 2:6) and this is a doctrine which Jesus repeatedly endorsed (Matthew 25:31-46; Luke 21:41-48; John 5: 25-29)

Then again, retribution is our only link with justice in this area, for it is asking what you have done and what you deserve, in deciding what is to be done about you. The other approaches can skip this questions and go straight to your thought-reform or to the good of the cause ('that the whole nation perish not', as Caiaphas remarked in deciding against Jesus).

But a frequent objection to retribution by human agent is that we are all guilty. True, we say, society must protect its self but if its starts paying back offenders in their or coin ('a tooth for a tooth') it has a wrong attitude altogether. Didn't Jesus say as much?

He did, but not to those who administer the law. He condemned the attitude of tit-for-tit, but he had no quarrel with a ruler's right to punish. The disciple, as Paul insists in Romans 12:19 must not pay back an injury, for retribution is God's affair. But it is also; he goes on, aruler's affair, indeed his duty, for God has delegated it to him. Romans 13:4 which makes this point, uses the same set of terms to speak up for public retribution (literally 'a retributor for wrath') as the earlier verses used against our private resort to it. (The NEB brings this out better than RSV.)

The next thing to ask is what penalty the Bible fixed for murder, and what force this may have now. The first part is soon answered. For mankind in general, from the days of Noah, God's rule was, 'Whoever sheds the blood of man, by man shall his blood be shed' (Genesis 9:6) the law of Moses reaffirmed it for Israel (Numbers 35:29-34), and the New Testament upheld the right of a state to enact it (Act 25:11; Romans 13:4).

But in answer to the second question, the civil laws of the Old Testament are not carried straight over into the new. They reveal unchangeable truths - in this case, the sanctity of life, the desert of a murderer, and society's duty to punish him - but they embody them in local regulations which are no longer binding on us just as they stand. So it is up to each state to create its own laws, but their values must stand the test of scripture.

With that in mind, we can-at last.-look at some pros and cons of capital punishment.

Strength And Weaknesses

Firstly let us take some points in its favour:

*   It is at least legitimate, perhaps even mandatory, being prescribed in the Old Testament and unquestioned in the New.
*   It is based on retribution, which is the biblical principle.
*   It puts a high value on the victim's life (Genesis 9:6b)
*   It is the strongest of deterrents (Deuteronomy 19v20) Against these we must place other consideration:
*   Many laws, appropriate once, are now outgrown and unthinkable. Slavery, though permitted rather than commanded, is one such death for adultery or for defiance of one's parents (Deuteronomy 21:18) is another. Should we not add to these, death for a murderer.
*   Even as retribution, this penalty is inexact, it is also irrevocable. Other sentences can much the degree of guilt, and be revoked if necessary. So justice itself, to say nothing of mercy, seems better served by other means than death.
*   The state's refusal to kill even the guilt declares the value it sets on all human life.
*   A deterrent effect is hard to prove or to isolate from other factors. And the drama of a death sentence can even attract same whom it should repel.

Personal View

Both positions have their strength and weaknesses. Both are defensible, and the changing state of the society may make one or the other the right choice for different times and places. To me, the balance falls in favour of including capital punishment in the range of sentences for the following reasons, corresponding to the pros and cons above.

Firstly, it is granted that many laws and customs are rightly left behind, yet the penalty for murder is in a special class in the Bible. It was a universal statute before it was an Israelite one (Genesis 9:6). The point is weakened by being true also of the food laws of Genesis 9:4. But the food laws were all replaced in the New Testament (1 Corinthians 10:25-27), whereas this was not, and then in Israelite law special reason were given for allowing nothing to replace it (Numbers 35:31). While this is far from conclusive, it makes one hesitate to ague from the disappearance of other institution to the abolition of this one.

Secondly, the existence of such a penalty does not banish mercy or restraint. This can be still exercised. As a matter of history as I discovered in my studies, nearly half the number of all convicted murderers in Great Britain in the first fifty years of the last century were reprieved from execution (Royal Commission Report on Capital Punishment)

Then, to argue that death for murder shows disregard for life, is as false as to say that imprisonment for kidnapping shows the disregard for liberty. Rather, the mild sentence is the one which tends to cheapen the offence in the eyes of society, by the comparisons it invites with other crimes and punishments.

Finally, for deterrence, as for anything else, cause and effect are notoriously hard to prove conclusively, but no one denies the phenomenal growth of violent crime in this continent and its various countries since the last 20 years or so. The new practice of classifying homicide as manslaughter wherever possible (on the plea of diminished responsibility) confuses the statistics but cannot hide the facts. We were assured that this explosion would not happen; we are now assured that it is a coincidence. I find this implausible, even when allowance has been made for contributory causes.

All in all, then, capital punishment is in my view certainly defensible, possibly dispensable in same societies, but eminently justified by scripture, reason and experience.

What about Advertisement?

For the life of me I cannot understand why advertising requires an apologia any more than the motor trade, the furniture industry, the rag trade and a host of others. No one is going to suggest that the motor trade has no rogues, that all furniture manufacturers produce higher quality merchandise or that same clothing is not rubbish, and he would be a fool who evenhoped that the methods of all advertisers could possibly be beyond reproach. There are good and bad Christians, but that does not mean the faith is suspect.

Now I am aware that there is a vocal minority holding the theory that in a correctly ordered state advertising in unnecessary. Yet despite its objection to the competitive economy, the fading Communist community Countries has introduced advertising because without it there was little incentive to raise production standards. The big mistake of the idealist is to forget that human nature is not 'ideal' and competition is essential and healthy for the human animal.

Advertisement Is Communication

Advertising assumes there is something to be communicated, whether in the promotion of ideas, persons or merchandise. It comes to us through posters, brochures, magazines, newspapers, cinema screens, TV, and radio, salesman at our doors, the church notice board, and the notice in church. All have something to say all sell. The first question must be, 'What is being promoted?' and the second, 'Should it be promoted at all?' This immediately takes the responsibility away from the advertising professional and places it squarely on the manufacturer. But who is going to be responsible for saying what is or is not to be produced? The total abstainer would say,' Ban or alcohol,' the non-smoker would feel the same about tobacco. Some folk would like to see all cars off the road etc., etc. Who is to decide?

Any activity-whether it be social, cultural, religious or economic within a human society is bound to be tainted with the sinfulness of those involved, Advertising is no exception. While it does not create the standards, it does mirror those already prevalent within society. Therefore I maintain if it is right to produce a product, then it is right to advertise it.

Advertisement and Society

The inventor inverts, the manufacturer takes the invention and with modern technology produces it for mass market, advertisement tell the public about the product and mass purchasing keeps the wheels of industry turning smoothly. If the invertors alone continued to produce small number of the product, the limited supply would make the unit cost phenomenal and the article would be available only to the rich, but the sterilizing of factory production lines makes the product available to the mass market at the price it can afford. This is not producing more materialism; it is merely making that which already exists available to more people. We have left behind the philosophy which says;

'The rich man in his castle, The poor man at his gate,
God made them high and lowly, And ordered their estate'.

It has been argued if the high cost of advertising was removed from the price of the product, merchandise would be cheaper; yet without advertising the consumer would never know about the product, and small demand would put us back to square one with a high- priced, consumed commodity. Mass markets require mass production and factories, and these must have workers, and workers rely on work for their own good standard of living. Advertising is vital to full employment in Africa.

Let us go back to that other point about advertising creating needs. No manufacturer would go into production without first testing the market. Research teams descend on a selected area where they expose the proposed product to the potential customers. Not until they are satisfied that an enthusiastic market exists and that the product is modified to conform to the requirement of that market, do they go into production. The need is already there and the advertisers discover that need.

Of course there are many similar products making claims to consumer benefits which often which sound extravagate. Variety provides us with a choice, and freedom of choice has always been a strong point in democracy. But much more than this, it saves the consumer from being exploited. Manufacturers are constantly analyzing their competitors 'production and trying to out-do each other. In this way the product is exploited, not the housewife, because she gets the benefits in improved products, and lower prices.

Stretching the Truth

It is absolutely essential that we retain our sense of honours where advertisements are concerned. There is little enough in life these days to make people laugh, why not take advertisement less seriously and enjoy them. Many do little more than leave us with a happy association with the subject. No one believes for a minute, that the clear, cool Heineken 'reaches the parts other beers cannot reach 'there by making the tired feet of the policemen wriggle, and the sparse foliage on the old dame's fancy hat develop into a veritable Africa Flower Show! We need to remember that much of the content of the advertisement is to gain our attention and make the product stay in our minds. And since we are going to buy one of the products anyway, good luck to the advertiser who creates the right atmosphere for his product. There are many people like me who laugh with the advertisement but are not sold by it – we just do not and will not drink lager.

Critics will say that some statements are made which are either misleading or down-right dishonest, making doubtful promises and offering misleading benefits to purchasers, Yet, it does sometimes happen, but any section of society is only good as the people who compose itor else there would be no need for rules, but it would be quite wrong to say that all advertisement are misleading. The Advertising Standards Authority has a comprehensive set of regulation which states that all advertising should be legal, decent, honest and truthful and that the code is to be applied not only in the letter, but in the spirit. Anyone suspecting an advertiser of making a dishonest claim can institute proceedings against the offender for violating the Trade Discriminations Act. The Broadcasting Authority exercises a true control on advertisements. Very few advertisers will risk their future and goodwill by going against this code of advertising practice. Also if advertisers indulge in dishonest methods of advertising and complaint is made to the Authority the newspaper or magazine concerned may refuse to accept further space booking from the advertising agency which placed the advertisement and that could put an agency out of business over-night. It just is not worth the risk.

The Hidden Urge

It has been suggested that advertising plays on people's fear, hopes and insecurities as a means to sell products; and it is only a short from this to say that human nature is exploited to make money. Here I believe we are playing with words. Does someone else always have to be blamed because I am human, have certain desires and attempt to fulfill them? Is it wrong to want to be warm in winter, have a comfortable home, and provide the best food and opportunities for my children? It is also felt that the alleged powerful techniques of persuasion used are dangerous because they play on our basic human nature, particularly where sex is concerned. Some advertisers do go too far in what they portray, yet nothing like as far as the rest of the media to which the guying public is exposed. Of course there are sometimes isolated sports of bad taste, but it would be unfair to claim that all advertising is so unhealthy.

Advertising does not function in a vacuum. The strange thing is that critics never see themselves as threatened by the techniques; rather they claim to be protecting someone else. The 'attention getter' may make us look at the product and we may even buy it, but if the product is not what we want, we will not buy it a second time. It is not unusual to hear the expression 'subliminal advertising used in connection with sales promotion. This kind of advertising is highly specialized, quite immoral, and comes pretty close to brain-washing, but happily is forbidden by law to be used in Britain, America and some European countries, but for us in Africa the dumping valley of the West anything goes.

The Christian Code

It is ridiculous for Christians to think they can impose their biblical standards on the advertising profession, any more than any other industry. But the Christian does have a role to play and responsibility to exercise in that part of the industry with which he or she is involved. It is wise to remember that while good laws are made, they are only so made because man is sinful and without them our society would be in anarchy. There are many secular rules controlling advertising practice, and these must be upheld.

The Bible teaches 'Provide things honest in the sight of all men,' 'Shun the appearance of evil and the Christian Advertiser will take extra care to sure this is carried out in his work. He will remember his weaker brother and this may mean that he will decline to handle certain products which violate his Christian conscience. There are many hinges which our society and culture permit which a Christian may have to think twice about in the light to Christ's teaching. We all have a responsibility to clean up our society where necessary. Christians have an added responsibility. The advertising profession is responsive to public opinion and if Christian devoted more of their energies to awaking the public opinion, this could achieve far more success than constantly complaining about the profession itself.

CHAPTER FOUR

POVERTY AND PAINS

We need to consider the suffering humanity. In many countries of the world it is the masses that bear the brunt of poverty, pains and oppressions. As a result, critical minds have asked and still asking vital questions regarding the state of the oppressed and afflicted. Below are vital critical queries and their answers:

Does God Really Care About Individual with Millions of People Living and Dying? There are really two questions here. There is the one on the surface, and there is the question beneath the question. The former asks whether God can care. And the answer 'Yes' can be given by the followers of the most religions who believes in a personal God of some kind, and even by those of no religion who accept that the world that we live in is the work of a being outside itself. If we say that such a God is infinite, it means that he is not limited by anything outside himself. And if he is infinite, he can be infinitely great as well as infinitely small. The God of the galaxies is also the God of the atom. To say this is to give an intellectual answer to an intellectual problem. But beneath the surface questions lies a deeper one. There is not only the problem of whether God can care, but whether he actually does care. Is God really concerned for the countless victims of atrocity and disaster that we calmly watch on our TV screen-and the millions more that we never see? To understand the Christian answer to this question we have got to look at it at long range and at short range. I mean asking what the Bible says about the care that God shows for us.

This world

What kind of the world is it that God has put us in? In a perfect machine nothing can go wrong. Every part has its place and function in the way that is designed to. But it has no choice. It cannot respond on its own initiative. It has no say in the matter. It just functions. But the kind of world that God has put us is not like that. God has paid man the intolerable compliment of handing over to him the choice of how he is to run his life. And with it he has created the possibility of making wrong and selfish choices.

Now this has bearing on the kind of care that God has for his creation. When the Bible talks about the love of God, nothing could be further from the 'smother love' that it always interfering. Real love is not giving the child everything that it wants on demand. The best gifts are those which enable the child to develop it faculties and grow as a person. And the best relationships are those which foster mutual response. But we cannot have it both ways. We cannot have situation in which God has given real freedom and responsibility to man to live and grow in mutual love and at the same time one in which God rushes in like an interfering grandmother whenever things go wrong.

Moreover, it is part of God's loving care that the laws of nature remain constant. The same fire that gives us warmth can also burn and destroy. The water that quenches thirst and is necessary to support life can also drown. We cannot expect God to bend the laws of nature every time we get in a jam. The kind of the world that God has put us is one in which we are able to use the things which belongs to it for good or ill. In a parish in which I once served we have a visiting card which said, 'The world is in a mess. But is it any wonder, if we neglect the maker's instruction? Part of the maker instruction is that we should love God with our whole being and our neighbours as ourselves (Matthews 22: 37ff; Mark12: 32ff; Luke10: 27ff). Part of God's care is to give us opportunity - and the obligation - to do just that.

Bible About God Concern

This brings us to what the Bible says about God's care for us. Its message is, in fact, double-edged. On the one hand, God cares in the sense that all men will have to give accountto him. If we neglect the physical laws of the universe, we can hurt ourselves and bring misery to others. The same applies to its spiritual laws. The apostle Paul put it this way: Do not be deceived, God is not mocked, for whatever a man sows that he will also reap (Galatians 6:7). Elsewhere he reminded his readers that we shall all appear before the judgment seat of Christ (2 Corinthians 5:10, Romans14:10 and Philippians 2:10). The same thought featured in the teaching of Jesus himself (Matthews 25:31-46). When someone pointed out a disaster which had befallen some people, thinking that it was a sign of God's judgment on them, Jesus replied, 'Unless you repent you will all likewise perish'(Luke13:3-5).

But God's care is not simply concerned with calling us to account. Just as the kind of world that God has put us in invites co-operation and trust between men, so the kind of relationship which God invites men to enter with him is one of co-operation and trust. He cares enough to send his son that whoever believes in him should not perish but have eternal life (John 3:16). Paul wrote: We know that in everything God works for good with those who love him, who are called according to his purpose (Romans 8:28). He went on to make it clear that this did not mean that we should be spared all pain and suffering. Indeed, it is sometime just the opposite. For Paul went on to list tribulation, distress, persecution, famine, nakedness, peril and the sword. It is in and through these things- when men do their worst and seem to be in complete control that God works and turns them into good with those who love him. In the same way Jesus spoke of the hairs of the disciple's head all being numbered and the sparrow not is falling to the ground without the father's will. (Matthews 10:20f; Luke12:3f). The experts of Jewish society in the in the first century tell us that the sparrow in question were not being sold as pets but to be killed as food for the poor. Even so, God is in control.

Something Deeper

This is one of the great paradoxes of the Christian faith. On one level, man seems to be in control and all events happen according to the laws of nature. But at the deeper level God is working in these events for the good of those who love him and trust him.

Yet the paradox does not stop there. For the good for which God is working may not always appear good at first sight. Although we are spared some pains and suffering, we are not spared all. There are things which in the last analysis are more important than physical well-being. What God cares about most is the kind of people that we turn out to be at the end of all these.

Pains and Sufferings

The first thing in tackling this question is to clarify what we mean by evil. Confusion here is common. I take the word here to mean badness of the moral sort- badness which here we recognize as good gone wrong and which we feel ought not to exist at all. Bad is also used, of course, in non-moral ways with such meanings as sub-standard, (e.g., a bad performance), unpleasant (e.g., a bad taste), or unhappy in its results (e.g., a bad move). but moral evil is different thing from these.

When you take a deep reflection on it, there are two kinds of things that we feel are morality bad. The first is the wrongdoings of moral agents, the badness of those who express vicious wills in vicious deeds. The second is pain and sufferings that seems unproductive, meaningless, and a waste of good so far as the sufferer is concerned. Evil of both kinds is felt as a problem; if God is really good and really almighty, how can he allow either to exist? We shall see the answer to this question later.

Purpose of Pain

To clear the ground, however, let it be said at once that not all pain is evil. Often pain is a needed warning, for if we should think thankful. When our hand hurts through inadvertent contact with a naked flame or boiling water, we are prompted to withdraw it at once- and a good thing too, if like lepers or those unhappy children who suffer from what doctors call congenital indifference to pain, we could not feel the hurt of our hand at such times, we should soon suffer fearful damage. So, too, it is a mercy when a pain in your head or your chest warns you that you are under strain and need a rest.

Similarly, physical suffering when bravery borne can produce nobility of character and a depth creativeness that would not be otherwise be there. Was Paul's thorn in the flesh an evil when it led him into a deeper experience of grace? (2 Corinthians 12:7-10)? Trouble has been called the chisel with which God sculpts our souls; it is no more morally evil than is the jarring of the nerve while the dentist drills your tooth.

Sin and Satan

But, granted all that, sin and much seemingly unproductive suffering remain. Where do these come from? There is mystery here, but the following points sum up as much as scripture tells us.

God is not the source of sin; he never commits, nor wills, nor prompts it. God cannot be tempted with evil and he himself tempts no one' (James 1:13). God made rational creatures who were capable of loving him freely and by choice and that meant that they could choose freely not to love him-which is what some angels and all our race have in fact done. Howsuch disobedience is possible, while God is Lord of his world (which scripture says he is), we cannot conceive; that it is possible is, however, undeniable, for it has happened.

If we ask how sin entered cosmos, scriptures replies Satan (the name means 'Adversary') and his angel rebelled against the creator before man was made (2 Peter 2:4, Jude 6). So that when the first human beings appeared 'that ancient serpent, who is the devil and Satan' (Revelation 20:2) was there to trip them up (Genesis 3). And the tempter' (1 Thessalonians 3:5), the 'ruler' and 'god' of this world, still marauds with serpentine cunning and lion-like savagery, seeking someone to devour' (1 Peter 5:8). It is right to trace moral evil back to Satan as its patron, promoter, producer, director and instigator cause.

But if the question is 'whence comes the inclination to evil which I find in myself and yield to so often', the Bible says the source is my own heart. Let no one say when he is tempted, "I am tempted by God;" … each person is tempted when he is lured and enticed by his own desire. Then desire when it has conceived gives birth to sin… (James 1:13). Jesus endorses this: Out of the heart of man come evil thoughts, fornication, theft, murder, adultery, converting, wickedness, deceit, licentiousness, envy, slander, pride, foolishness. All these evil things come from within …' (Mark 7:21). My 'heart' in biblical usage is the core of my personal being, the centre and root of the real 'me'. And what these passengers tell me is that, just like a cripple's twisted leg makes him walk lame, so the motivational twist of my fallen heart – anti-God anti-others, self-absorbed – constantly induces wrong attitudes and actions. Nor can I excuse these because they are inevitable (though they are), but I must acknowledge them in every case as my own fault, for, in the ordinary everyday sense of the phrase, my heart is in them. My wrong-doing originates in me, in that twist of nature which we call original sin.

If, now, our enquiry moves on from human sin to human suffering, the following thing may be said.

First, scripture sees the whole cosmos as cursed and out of joint. This curse is part of God's just judgment on human sin (Genesis 3:17; Romans 3:19-23). The creation has been subjected to 'futility' (i.e. non-achievement of its end, failure to achieve any worthwhile end at all). We are not told in detail what this subjection involved but it is natural to suppose that, just as physical death in the in the form in which we know it belong to the curse (Genesis 3:3; 19, Romans 6:23), so death dealers like cancer would not be as they are, were it not for the curse. The curse is one source, then of pain and of sickness. And for those who are not Christian there is no final remedy. Secondly, Christians follow Jesus, who endured 'from sinners such as hostility against them, as against their master, spring from the adverse reaction of sin-twisted nature to godliness in others-a reaction which is regularly destructive in intent. Here is the second source of suffering in this world.

Third, God is training all his children to enjoy a future life in which it is promised that tears and tribulation will be the thing of the past (Revelation 7:14-17; Hebrews 12 :2). Whatever we find ourselves experiencing, therefore, of the curse of creation or hostility to the godly, should be thought of as part of the present discipline whereby God teaches us patience, courage, humility, faithfulness and similar lessons, and as originating in his own plan for our sanctification.

Fourth, whatever perplexity may remain as to why this or that form of evil touches our lives, we should realize that what God in sovereign goodness did through Jesus' life, death and resurrection to handle and overcome evil, with a view to eliminating it eventually from his world; and that what, in the same sovereign goodness, he want us to learn is not primarily how to explain evil, but how to handle and overcome it for ourselves in Jesus power/Name. What matters is less that we should know its source than that we should know that God is now dealing with it to dispel it and we should be his mouth piece here to overcome for him in Jesus Name.

The Plight of the Third World

What Should Christian Do About The Plight Of The Poor In Our Society And other Parts Of The World

The Bible says that it is God's gift to man that everyone should eat and drink (Ecclesiastes 3:13) yet tonight half of the people living in our world will go to bed hungry. And tomorrow 15,000 people will literally starve to death. That is the daily death total of people who die of hunger. Why, when for the first time in human history we have we have means to feed all mankind? I think President Kennedy put the answer in the sentence: 'We lack only the willingness to share.'

To start with those neat little economic labels that split mankind into separate segments reflect in themselves our selfishness and greed. For instance, 25% of the world's population enjoy and exploit 75% of the world's wealth and natural resources. Meanwhile the three- quarters of the world's population – the so-called third World – eke out their existence on the remaining 25% of the world's wealth.

Now in considering the plight of the Third World there is the tendency to feel overwhelmed by the enormity of its problem. Bombarded by reports through the press, Radioand Television, there is a temptation to switch off or' do an ostrich' in order to maintain our sanity. Perhaps we feel like Roberts Louis Stevenson when he wrote:

- **The World is so big and I am so small,**
- I do not like it at all, at all.

But as Dr Schumacher, one of the world's leading economists, states, 'Small is beautiful.' In other words the smaller the project or programmed the more likely its success and in the most underdeveloped regions of Africa, Asia and Latin America the Christian Church has proved this simple theory in setting up model agriculture units, public health programmed, trade training schools, etc. together national Christians, missions and Christians agencies such as our own, have seeing this thesis in action; small is both beautiful and meaningful. It provides help for the present and offers hope for the future. And it helps people to help themselves, which, in the long run, is the most effective form of assistance that anyone can be given.

Nevertheless there are those who ask, 'But why do you bother? The needs are overwhelming and your resources are totally inadequate. It's just a drop in the ocean'. Maybe. But as it has been said, 'the ocean is made up of many drops,' Mother Theresa Calcutta shares a similar statement with Malcolm Muggeridge in his book Something Beautiful for God. We ourselves feel that what we are doing is just a drop in the ocean. 'But if that drop was not in the ocean I think the ocean would be less because of that missing drop'. Besides, the fact that I cannot do everything is no reason why I shouldn't do anything. So what am I as a Christian called to do?

Responding To the Need

Firstly, am called to aware – to be aware of the needs of the world in which I live and to be aware of my responsibility in helping to meet some of those needs.' It is the task of the Christian man and Christian society, 'says Michael Green in his book Jesus Spells Freedom 'both to keep informed as to what is threatening the world and to press for truly human priorities to be kept uppermost in national and international policies.' This kind of awareness will govern the way I vote at the elections, determined my life style, clarify my priorities and give me more realistic scenes of perspective. It could even give me a new sense of vocation and alter all my direction in life.

In an all-out attempt to foster and increase this awareness most Christian's agencies use a whole range of publications and educational aids

Called To Care Secondly, we are called to care. 'If a mother cares', runs the Seven Up commercial, 'the different is clear.' And if we as Christians care – the different must be clear. 'Little children,' write the apostle John, 'let us stop just saying we love people, let us really love them and show it by our actions' (1 John 3:18, Living Bible). For some, this could possibly lead to personal service in the mission's field. It's a salutary thought that you could be the answer to somebody's prayer for meeting a need that God wants to meet through you. Maybe God is waiting to express his love and care through you in our continent, Asia or Latin America.

I once heard that in Bangladesh one of the NGO nurses sitting at supper after a particularly harrowing day in the refugee camps. 'I wonder at times', she said, 'if God really cares for the people that are there.' It was a question born out of watching relentless suffering and hardship. But with great presence of mind a senior missionary said quietly, 'Yes he cares. And you are there because God cares.' And it could be that God may want you there as an expression of his care.

Called To Share

Thirdly, we are called to share. In the last chapter of the epistle to the Hebrews, the iter encouraged his leader to offer up through Jesus 'a sacrifice of praise to God, that is, the fruit of lips that acknowledge his name' (13:15). But, as the old prayer puts it, this praise is not only to be declared with our lips; it must also be demonstrated in our lives. This inter- relation becomes self-evident in Hebrews 13 when the message goes on to say, 'Do not neglect to do well and to share what you have, for such sacrifices are pleasing to God; (16).

Remember that incidents early in the Gospel when the people came to John the Baptist with the desire to make amends. 'What are we to do then?' they ask, and you will recall the answer: 'whoever has food must share it' (Luke 3:10-11). If then as Christians we really care, it will be shown by the extent in which we are prepared to share with others what we ourselves so richly enjoy. For, as sent John says, 'If anyone has the world's goods and sees his brother in need yet closes his heart against him, how does God's love you abide in him?'(1John3:17).

Burden of Prayer

Fourthly, I am called to bear part of burden of prayer for my Continent.' Art thou weak and heavy laden, 'runs the old hymn, 'cumbered with a load of care?' in times of personal temptation, difficulties we rejoice at being able to follow the hymn writer's advice and 'take it to the Lord in prayer. 'But we must learn to widen the scope of this petition if we are prayerfully to bear the burdens of our World. Each night after watching the news report on American television I learnt that Bill Graham and his wife switch off and bow in prayer to God for the places and the people they have just been watching.

It's a good start. 'Pray much for others,' says Apostle Paul, 'plead for God's mercy upon them gives thanks for all he is going to do for them' (1 Timothy 2:1, Living Bible). For a Christian, this is one of our highest calling and ultimately one of our most meaningful contributions in co-operating with God for meeting the needs in his world.

CHAPTER FIVE

DRUG ABUSE

Whenever the subject of drugs use is mentioned there is a tendency first of all for us to think of same type of young person's problem involving the taking of illicit drugs. The issue for the Christian is much broader than this.

Can A Christian Use Drug?

Christian's Response to Drug In Society.

First, we have to recognize that we are living in God's world, and his scheme of things includes the beneficial use of drugs. Many of the scientists who discover drugs were Christians. We are abusing God's gifts just as much if we take the 'head in sand' attitude of
'I'm not taking anything at all.'
Secondly, we need to plan how we are going to take drugs. We each need our own pattern. Are we going to take drugs just when they are prescribed? Are we going to drink or smoke? What controls we are going to put over our drug setting?

Drug and the Society

As far as we can tell mankind has been using drugs since earliest times, finding potions to heal the body kill the diseases, or change the state of the mind. Our society has developed its chemical technology considerations and we are able to benefit from all manner of drugs which both ease pain and combat disease. If we compare our life with a condition of the century ago we can see the tremendous benefit that drugs have brought to society today. At the same time we have to be aware of the fact that we seem to be able to do less with stress and anxiety and same drugs are an easy and effective way of blotting out reality, if only temporarily. By far the majority of drugs act as selective poisons. They do not produce the miraculous reaction by adding something to the body. Instead, they kill of something which has entered the system or else poison the activity of one part of the body in such a way as to aid the remainder of it. If they are used indiscriminately they can cause short or long term problem or dependence (once called addiction).

In Zambia for example, we control most drugs so that only doctors can prescribe most of them. A doctor is able to decide the correct dose, the period of time for which the chemical can be given and possible side effects. This system is open to abuse where a patient pressurizes the doctor for drugs for conditions which could be treated in other ways.

Another group of drugs which can be prescribes by doctors, together with same substances with no medical use, are controlled under the Drug Misuse Act. These drugs are sold illicitly by various people who are either addicted themselves or who make a profit from the sale of drugs. Because of the damage they can cause to the individual, and the ability of people to pressurize others to use them, passion of and trading in these drugs and their use is punishable by fine or imprisonment. In this group are various sedatives and stimulants narcotics (drugs derived from or similar to opium) and substances which change the functioning of the mind like the hallucinogens (LSD) and cannabis (pot).

A third group of drugs could be described as store drugs. These are the countless substances sold over the counter for every conceivable minor ailment. Some can be very useful, like aspirin, but others are of more dubious worth, and during the last decade there has been a sharp increase in the availability and sale of such substances. There has been a growth too in the number of people who now take something for the slightest ache or pain

Yet another group of drugs consists of those classed as socially acceptable. In Zambia, caffeine which is found in tea and coffee does little harm unless people take excessive doses. However another acceptable drug, nicotine, is considered responsible for the death of 2,000 to 5,000 people every year. Alcohol does not kill people in the same numbers or the same way but is responsible for large numbers of road accident and is acknowledged as a major causative factor in the levels of crime, violence etc. We have developed a society where few people are objective about their own drinking habits and where we have about many million alcoholics.

The Effects of Drug Abuse

Controlling use and abuse of drug is demanded because of its abuse and side effects. If we consider any drug that we are going to use, the circumstances we are using it in and the reason for use we should think carefully about the following:

What are its immediate effects?

Will it affect the way my mind or body function and make me any the less able to respond to doing God's will or make me more prone to damaging myself or others? As Christians we see our minds and bodies as gifts from God, to be used for him and at any time available his use.

Is it possible that a habit may build up by the use of this drug?

If so could that harm my body or mind in the future? (2 Corinthians 3:16-18; 1 Corinthians 6:19; 2 Corinthians 6:16)

Will it make me behave any differently from normal?

As Christians we are called to be in control of all of our faculties. (Romans 6:13; 2 Peter 3:17).

Could this drug, in the way I am using it, cause addiction?

Addiction takes away all self-control. Behaviour of this sort is in complete opposition to the Christian's understanding of conduct. (Proverbs 20:1; Isaiah 5:11; Luke 21:34)

Am I respecting the opinions of others?

By taking a drug in a particular setting you may inconvenience others or make it difficult for others to stick to their principles.

What example am I selling to others?

We need to be conscious of the fact that even if we believe we are able to be responsible in our use of one type of drug, another person following our example may be totally unable to control its use. (Romans 14 especially v. 10, 13, 14, 19, 21. see also the table at the end of this chapter).

Drug: Any Short Term or Long Term Problem?

Normally the doctor will warn if there is any danger. E.g. if there are warnings on tables: 'do not drive whilst using drugs', if heeded, no problems. The doctor is able to decide when to stop so as to prevent long term problems. Some people take so many that they slowly poison the body.

Tobacco: Causes considerable predisposition nicotine to lung cancer, other cancers, bronchitis, and thrombosis. In majority, it creates inconvenience to others. Smokers will shorten life span and impair body reactions and health after period of time.

Alcohol: It slows down the brain after taking. Excessive regular use damages organs particularly stomach and liver. Alcoholic person are therefore more prone to road accident or other accidents. The person loses inhibitions, also becomes over confident and then there is tendency for people to relax their limits once affected by alcohol. Affects brain for considered time (one pint for three hours though this does very). Heavy dose can course sleep or death.

Illicit drugs: Barbiturates slow brain, easy to take overdose, make the user more prone to accidents. Easy to became addicted by long term use, Tendency to increase dose.

Stimulants: Side effects of tensions and exhaustion, easy progression to regular use with strong psychological (mind) dependence.

Hallucinogens: (LSD} The taker does not know what he is doing or what is really happening. It causes mental disorientation or occasional physical harm by inducing around him accident. It can bring out latent mental problems.

Cannabis: Slows down brain, makes a person very subjective to experience accident if driving. Psychological dependence, bring out latent problem in some.

Narcotics: Slows brain, easy for overdose. Overdoses cause numerous physical complications. Will it charge behavior? Will it charge addiction?

If a particular drug is going to make a person to be depressed or moody the doctor will normally prevent this. Only if the patient pressures warn about this, the doctor knows when to stop the drug. For some type of drugs can this occur?

* If used in large quantities and poisoning occurs then irrational behaviour may result
* If a person uses them automatically rather than specific ailments (carefully obeying instructions) psychological addiction can occur.*If a person tries to give up smoking, he may find it hard or else become tense when he cannot smoke. Some people are addicted to the nicotine in tobacco and cannot stop smoking.

Alcohol prevents clear thinking. In some people it will make them perform act they would not. A considerable amount of alcoholism has (very fell are down and outs) two danger signs: one, people drinking excessively normally commit crime, violence, wife and child-beating and themselves up or deal with stress; two, people drinking to alleviate tensions bolster neglect precipitated by alcohol. As the brain is slowed down, there is no way to be certain alcohol will not charge behaviour.

Strongly Addictive

Firstly, strongly addictive people start to rely on drugs. The user becomes progressively drug orientated. The user becomes very subjective in viewing drug experience. Sometimes he loses touch with reality. The experience becomes addictive. Those who use this become introspective. Psychological dependence can occur. The user becomes totally drug orientated, strongly addictive. Secondly, with illicit drugs a further complication is that there is no complete control over what the substance is - its purity, dosage or effects on my individual.

Thirdly, and most important, we need to think about situations in which we may find ourselves, where we will be asked to modify our drugs taking. For instance, if you decide not to drink, how will you react at the party when only alcohol is available? Or, if you set a certain limit on drinking soda alone, how do you react to your friend who pressurizes you to drink more than your limit? Then suppose you decide a Christian cannot take a illicit drugs; how will you react when you find yourself at a company were cannabis is being passed around? Again you must feel tense (and it is quite respectable for Christians to feel like this). Will you take a tranquillizer or how else will you react?

Finally, the Christian has a tremendous contribution to make to society in helping those affected by drugs. Working with drug addicts is not glamorous, contrary to the picture put around at times. It is an extremely hard field, but one in which practical help can be given. The contact with the person affected by drugs is of great importance in aiding him to gain a concept of himself as a person who matters to God, and who can be cured from his dependency by experiencing the deepest healing of personality which is to be found only in Christ. Any Christian Church or group can seek to support people with chemically orientated problem and become a loving caring community when the out casts feel they belong. We must never give glib answer to their problems, or when they sleep back, but must accept them as they are, as people suffering from a several illness. If they slip buck again and again, we need to remember that this does not mean they are any less Christian. It just means that we are Christians are not caring enough to give them the support to persevere.

BIBLIOGRAPHY

William Barclay; Ethics in a Permissive Society: London, Fontana Books, 1971

John Davidman; Smoke on the Mountain: London, Hoder and Stoughton, 1966

David Field; Taking Side: London; Inter – Varsity Press, 1975

Tony Cummings, Steve Goddard and Gill Smith. 20th Century Sex: UK Word Publishing, 1986

Tom Bathgate. So What's Next? UK OM Publishing. 1992

Johnson. F. Odesola, Keys To a Happy Marriage: Nigeria. 2000

AUTHOR'S CONNECTS

If you have been blessed by this message, you can also contact: Pastor Johnson Funso Odesola @ Redeemed Christian Church of God Headquarters, Ebute Mata, Lagos, Nigeria

Phone: +2348035361325; +2348074368534

Email:odesolajf@gmail.com; funsoodesola@yahoo.com
Follow me on Twitter: http://twitter.com/PastorJFOdesola
Friend me on Facebook: http://facebook.com/
PastorJFOdesola http://Youtube.com/ PastorJFOdesola
Follow me on Linkedin: http://ng,Linkedin.com/in/ PastorJFOdesola

Favorite me on Smashwords: http://www.
smashwords.com/profile/view/funsoodesola

Printed in the United States
By Bookmasters